This book inspired, challenged and motivated me – often all at once. I wholly commend it as a must-read for anyone who cares about seeing the world transformed.
Gavin Calver, Youth for Christ

Profoundly challenging – I would urge you to read this important book.
Rob Parsons, Founder and Chairman, Care for the Family

What's so good about the good news? For the answers to this and many other questions about what it means to see, know and follow Jesus in the twenty-first century, read on . . .
Russell Rook, CEO of Chapel Street and Chair of Spring Harvest Theme Group

Chick Yuill combines passion, wisdom, common sense and fun in this warm and wide-ranging book. He gives us a vision of following Jesus which is true to Scripture and spot on for our age. He has the happy knack of putting things freshly, making us see and think differently, and capturing our hearts and imaginations, as well as our minds. Several times I found myself saying, 'That's so true!' and was stirred with hope and a resolve to act. This book has the potential to reshape the church to make a real difference in our society.
John Valentine, Church Planter and author of Follow Me *(IVP)*

Moving in the Right Circles

Chick Yuill

Moving in the Right Circles

Embrace the discipleship adventure

ivp

INTER-VARSITY PRESS
Norton Street, Nottingham NG7 3HR, England
Email: ivp@ivpbooks.com
Website: www.ivpbooks.com

First published 2011

British Library Cataloguing in Publication Data
A catalogue record for this book is available from the British Library.

ISBN: 978-1-84474-503-6

Set in Dante 12/15pt
Typeset in Great Britain by CRB Associates, Potterhanworth, Lincolnshire
Printed and bound in Great Britain by Ashford Colour Press Ltd, Gosport,
Hampshire

*Inter-Varsity Press publishes Christian books that are true to the Bible and that
communicate the gospel, develop discipleship and strengthen the church for its mission
in the world.*

*Inter-Varsity Press is closely linked with the Universities and Colleges Christian
Fellowship, a student movement connecting Christian Unions in universities and
colleges throughout Great Britain, and a member movement of the International
Fellowship of Evangelical Students. Website: www.uccf.org.uk.*

Contents

Foreword   9

Up, up and away?   13

Walking in the company of Jesus

1. Invitation   23
2. Crucifixion   35
3. Imitation   49
4. Incarnation   63

Growing in the community of believers

5. A worshipping community   79
6. A dying community   95
7. A learning community   109
8. A witnessing community   123

Engaging with the culture of the times

9. Engaging intelligently   141
10. Engaging Christianly   155

Looking to the coming of the King

11. What will be, will be   171

Notes   187

Foreword

Of Tuareg fires, whole life and a Scottish rebel
I don't know if Chick has travelled much in his life.

I know he's lived in California and I'm pretty sure he's been to Croydon, but I have no idea if he has watched the sun set behind Everest, heard the Pacific lap gently up the platinum sands of Tahiti or caught the acrid scent of Tuareg campfires in the central Saharan wind. But you can tell from this book that he's been somewhere special. And that he's stayed there long enough to know that you can find it anywhere. And thought about it carefully enough to help others know how to get there.

This is a book about the realm of the real.

About what a life following Jesus looks like. It's not a fantasy story or an almanac for supersaints or a champions' guide to überholiness; it's a book about whole-life discipleship, about what it takes to live well for Christ in the realm of the real.

And every page has the ring of authenticity about it.

Chick recognizes the challenges of living as a Christian in a bewildered and anxious secular society, but he is also confident in the resources that Jesus offers. He knows that many churches are not what they might be but that none of us can become what God intended unless we are part of one. He acknowledges that Christian culture has too often – for centuries actually – ignored the places where people spend most of their time – work, school, clubs – but he's neither bitter nor cynical and can see ways for us to work together to change that. And to change those places and, more importantly, to be part of seeing other people come to know the transforming impact of knowing and following Jesus.

For in the realm of the real, real, ordinary people are transformed by Jesus. In the realm of the real, the Jesus we follow leads us to others who don't know him. This is his way. Indeed, this book never loses sight of the big picture, of the extraordinary scope of the gospel. It is good news for the poor, the least and the lost, as well as for the rich, the powerful and the self-confident. It is good news for business and politics and media as well as for education and health and social services

There is no nook of God's world where Jesus cannot make a difference, no person who would not benefit now and eternally from knowing him. Indeed, Chick has worked among the very poor, among the least and among those seemingly abandoned by society. He's also worked among the rich, the powerful and the self-confident. But because Chick has lived long in the realm of the real he doesn't ask us to live his life again for him, but rather to live the one Jesus calls us to where we are now.

If all that sounds rather earnest, this book isn't. Yes, it's purposeful and sometimes poignant but there's a spring in its step and joy at its heart. And when I got to the end, a film and a word came to mind.

The film was *Braveheart*, the not entirely accurate portrayal of the Scottish patriot William Wallace who, in the film at least, fought long, hard, brilliantly and self-sacrificially to throw off the English yoke. Wallace loved his people and saw his status as a way to serve them, not as a road to riches or self-aggrandizement. In the end he was betrayed and executed. His last word, in the film at least, expressed what he had fought for, and what even death could not take away: 'Freedom'.

That's what this book left me with – the sense that following Jesus as Lord and Master, doing what he says, in his ways, is the most extraordinary liberation. Freedom indeed.

It's something to be grateful for. As is this book. As is Chick.

Mark Greene
Executive Director
The London Institute for Contemporary Christianity
March 2011

Up, up and away?

The rock concert

The band was really good – and really loud! – and the place was literally rocking as hundreds of young people danced and swayed to the heavy, driving rhythm of the music. The full lighting rig, the powerful PA system and the arresting visual images on the large screens on either side of the stage said it all. This was a thoroughly professional gig, carefully constructed and superbly presented with its audience of teenagers very much in mind. I was considerably older than most of the audience, but not too old to appreciate that the members of the band had mastered their craft. They knew how to play their music. And I was all the more intrigued because the four talented musicians on stage were committed Christians whose sole reason for making music, they explained to their enthusiastic audience, was to share their joy at being followers of Jesus.

I couldn't help but admire their passion for evangelism and their skill in communicating their faith in a musical language that was cringe-free and culturally relevant to their generation. But then the music stopped and everything went quiet, or at least as quiet as it can ever be with over five hundred hot and sticky young people crowded in front of a stage. It was time to be serious, time to talk about why we were there, *time for the altar call*. And these guys were not beating around the bush. They got straight to the point: we've all done bad stuff and deserve to be punished by God, but Jesus has died for us and paid the price of our sins.

Then they cast the net out. With the house lights now turned up, the lead singer looked across the entire crowd and made the challenge. It was loud and clear and I remember it word for word: 'So, guys, come and get your sins forgiven, become mates with God, and get to go to the big party in heaven. If you're up for that, raise your hand and we'll pray for you.'

That was it. Some seventy or eighty kids raised their hands, and after a prayer from the stage, they were led into an anteroom for counselling and follow-up. I was left standing there pretending to pray, but not knowing whether to cry tears of frustration or to call out, 'Don't do it, kids. That's not the real deal at all!'

The real deal

I didn't do either of those things. I just went home and sat up late into the night reflecting on what a poor job my own generation had done in passing on the gospel to a group of gifted and sincere rock-musician evangelists. For they were, after all, simply repeating in the idiom of their generation a formula that has been rehearsed many times over many years in the more formal jargon of church-speak. It's a formula that has reduced the gospel to little more than a guaranteed safe passage to heaven. And, of course, that's part of the truth. The gospel *does* give us an assurance that our sins are forgiven and a firm hope of a life that is greater than death.

But to stop there misses the point of it all. When we acknowledge Jesus as Saviour and Lord we are doing much more than obtaining a passport into heaven. We are enlisting in a project that will involve us in working to bring the rule of God to every situation, a project which aims at nothing less than the renewal of the creation for which Jesus died and for which his resurrection is the promise of ultimate transformation. Alas, all too often Christians have been fixated on travelling to the next world as quickly as possible when they should have been focused on the task of transforming this world for as long as they live.

We have done less than justice to the message that Jesus proclaimed and to the call that he sounded to would-be disciples. Rather than inviting them to be 'up, up and away' – to make their getaway while the world goes to hell in a handcart – he was in fact commissioning them to make a difference here and now. He intended his own life, death and resurrection to be the template for his followers. They too must live in obedience to the Father. They too must give their lives for the sake of the gospel and a lost world. And they too must bring the power of the resurrection to every seemingly hopeless life and every apparently desperate situation.

Their decision to follow Jesus was not intended to be the starting point for an odyssey that would get them from this world to the next. Instead, as they walked in his company, that was to be the *centre* from which they would move out in ever-widening circles. From there they were to grow in maturity in the community of their fellow believers, and engage meaningfully and redemptively with the culture that surrounded them. They were to do all this in the confidence that the One who had called them, who was crucified for them and who had conquered death itself, would one day come again as Lord and King. His coming would be to establish once and for all his rule of love and justice over all the world. So they were not to retreat from the world. Rather, they were to move through it with a reckless abandon. They were to establish the Lordship of Jesus in every area of life as they declared the gospel story by their words and demonstrated the good news by their deeds.

The resurrection adventure

Following Jesus is much more than just journeying to heaven. It is, in fact, to begin to understand our calling and to play our part in initiating and establishing God's completed miracle of redemption into which all our present efforts will be gathered up.

It was my friend Phil who, for me, expressed the link between the often painful exertions of the here and now and the wonderful consummation of the age to come. Phil's wife Nicola had fought a magnificent and moving fight against cancer. Her firm faith simply served to highlight the truth that sickness is an intruder in God's world. Her unwavering commitment to serve others was a declaration that even the darkest situations can be transformed. When Nicola died, Phil sent a text message to all his friends which said simply but perceptively, 'Nicola died peacefully at 6 o'clock this evening to continue her resurrection adventure.' That's it exactly. The gospel is not a call to escape, but a commissioning to a glorious, never-ending adventure in which we have a part to play in God's great strategy to make all things new. It's an adventure that begins the moment we respond to Jesus, that continues all through this life, and is gloriously fulfilled in the life to come.

The right place to begin

There are countless people today who are disillusioned by what they know of Christianity and what they see of the church. They think of it – often with good reason – as a tired institution, shut away in half-empty buildings, anchored to the past, bound by rigid dogma and providing a suitable refuge only for those weary souls who've given up on life. But the same people are often drawn almost irresistibly to Jesus. Instinctively they recognize that this is a man whose life and teaching challenge us to discover a purpose and pattern that makes life worth living. Most of those people have never been part of the church. Others continue to attend, but are just hanging on wondering whether it's worth the effort. It's especially for people like this – people who are drawn to Jesus but who are tempted to despair of the church – that this book has been written.

What follows is an attempt to centre everything on the call of Jesus, the invitation to know him and to follow him as his disciples. But discipleship is not membership in an emergency plan for the safe evacuation of the faithful to 'a better place'. Rather, discipleship is enlisting in God's resurrection project for the world that he created. It is a world that he sustains by his word of power, that he loved enough to die for, and that he will one day heal from every hurt and wound.

So, please read on. But be warned – if you take his challenge seriously it will be no easy ride. It will be gruelling as well as glorious. It will, in truth, cost you everything. But it will be the best bargain you ever made . . .

Going Deeper

1. If you are already a committed Christian, how does the way in which the Christian gospel was presented to you influence your understanding of what it means to be a follower of Jesus?

2. In what ways has that positively impacted your life as a disciple? And are there any negative effects?

3. If you have not yet made that commitment, are there any aspects of the way in which Christians have presented their beliefs to you that have discouraged or hindered you from becoming a follower of Jesus?

Walking in the company of Jesus

1. Invitation

Starting from the wrong place

To say that I was surprised to be invited to appear on *The Jeremy Kyle Show* on daytime TV would be an understatement. For anyone who doesn't know, he's Britain's answer to America's Jerry Springer, and the show's unashamed agenda is simply to encourage the participants to share the lurid details of the less attractive side of their family life with the general public. In return they receive some of the host's homespun, if somewhat questionable, wisdom. As often as not, the protagonists end up having to be restrained from indulging in something akin to a bare-knuckle boxing match. However, after being informed of the subject for that day, I agreed to appear on the show. It turned out to be an interesting experience.

The producers had arranged a live link with three members of a church in America's Midwest which has gained notoriety for two things. They fly all over the States in order to demonstrate at the funerals of American service personnel who have been killed on active service; their protest takes the form of carrying placards aggressively declaring their conviction that the deaths of these young men and women represent a judgment from God on their country. And they are virulently and notoriously anti-gay. To make that point clear, the three church members on the live link that day were wearing black T-shirts with the legend in bold white lettering: 'GOD HATES FAGS'.

Worse was yet to come. Following the opening credits there was a video clip of the founder of the church speaking a couple of years before, just days after a campus shooting in the States in which thirty students had been killed. 'We rejoice in those deaths,' he said. 'They represent God's judgment on America. Our only regret is that it wasn't 30,000 people killed.' I took a deep breath, offered up a quick prayer, and hoped that I might say something that would convince the audience that Christianity, insensitivity and insanity were not interchangeable terms!

There were three of us on the panel in the studio that day. On my right was a woman whose son had been killed on active service in Iraq. The black-shirted church members told her that her son was cursed by God and was certainly now in hell. On my left was a young man who was the publicity officer for the Lesbian and Gay Foundation in the north-west of England. I don't ever want to repeat what they said to him. And there in the middle was me, trying to bring some sanctified sanity and genuine Christian compassion to the debate.

I couldn't do anything else but question the angry denunciations of these censorious followers of Christ. 'Aren't you being excessively judgmental?' I dared to ask. 'Surely the gospel teaches that God loves *all* sinners?'

They turned on me with a venom that was quite unnerving. 'No, you're wrong!' they shouted. 'God hates us until we repent. Only then does he start to love us.'

That's when I realized how they could have such a distorted view of the Christian faith. *They had started at the wrong place.* Their theology began with divine judgment and then called for human repentance in order to win God's favour and approval. They totally ignored the fact that it's only God's love and grace that makes such repentance possible.

Of course, I've taken an extreme example. But here's the really worrying thing. As the discussion widened out to involve the members of the studio audience, it became all too clear that many of them thought that the angry judgmentalism of the guests from across the Atlantic was characteristic of all Christians. Little wonder then that the Christian gospel is failing to make an impact on people for whom it has such negative connotations. And what if there is even just a modicum of truth in their perception of what Christians believe? We can protest that their understanding is skewed and their verdict unfair as much as we like – but the little they've observed of our witness and the less they've seen of our worship have conveyed something quite different from what our words attempt to communicate. Could it be, in fact, that we have all too often started from the wrong place, not only in our thinking on mission and discipleship, but in our understanding of the gospel itself?

Ian is in his late fifties. Despite growing up in a Christian family, he has no contact with church, other than attending weddings and funerals. He describes himself as still holding to many of the values he learned as a child – honesty, faithfulness in marriage, compassion for the poor. But he doesn't trust religion. On the few occasions when he speaks about the matter, he refers to his childhood experience of Sunday School.

'They used to teach us a chorus which they made us sing most weeks: "He sees all I do, He hears all I say, My God is writing all the time, time, time . . . " I hated that chorus. And I didn't like the idea of a God like that who snooped on kids instead of getting on with looking after the universe and putting right the injustices of the world. I still don't like the thought of a God like that. So church is not for me.'

Going back to the beginning

It's time to follow the wise counsel of Maria to the von Trapp children in *The Sound of Music*:

> Let's start at the very beginning,
> A very good place to start . . .

In fact, it's time to go right back to the Gospels and to the dramatic sentences with which Mark introduces the public ministry of Jesus: 'After John was put in prison, Jesus went into Galilee, proclaiming the good news of God. "The time has come," he said. "The kingdom of God is near. Repent and believe the good news!"' (Mark 1:14–15)

Time change

When you set them in the context of their time, Mark's words are startling and unsettling. Clearly Galilee under the reign of Herod Antipas, a particularly unpleasant and unpredictable ruler, was an unpromising setting for establishing new ministries! John the Baptist's prophetic challenge resulted in his imprisonment and impending execution. But no sooner is he incarcerated in Herod's dungeon than Jesus appears on the scene to launch his campaign. Not great timing, it would seem! Either Jesus is consumed with a self-destructive urge that has rendered him oblivious to the consequences of his actions, or else he's carrying an urgent message whose time has come and which will brook no delay.

Mark is in no doubt that it's the second of these possibilities that drives Jesus on. The urgency of his mission is expressed in a succinct message: *The time has come.* Those simple but powerful words are not just the beginning of Mark's account of the life of Jesus. They seem to be written large over every genuine encounter that human beings have had with Jesus across the centuries. *This is a man to be reckoned with and, if you take him seriously, everything changes from that point onwards.* It's no coincidence that we date our calendars from the coming of Jesus. Things are never going to be the same again! When you decide to follow him, it doesn't really feel like converting to a new religion. It's much more like entering – or maybe, more accurately, like being engulfed by – a whole new reality. Whenever he appears on the scene, everything changes. You cross a threshold into a brand-new kind of living.

Good news

Eddie and Joe are gay. Over the years they have attended a number of different churches. They didn't usually stay too long. When the rest of the congregation found out about their sexual orientation, they felt less than welcome.

Now they're attending a church where one of the members has taken a special interest in them. She says, 'They're sinners just like me and the first thing they need to hear is not someone condemning their lifestyle, but a fellow sinner telling them that God loves all of us, whoever and whatever we are, and wants the best for us. Of course, when we meet in our small group we try to examine what the Bible says about how we should live. But we emphasize that we're all a work in progress and we're all in need of forgiveness.'

Eddie and Joe have stayed longer than they ever have done in any previous church.

The content and tone of Jesus' message highlight the radical change ushered in by his breaking onto the scene. Although his summons carried implications of God's judgment, it was unlike John's preaching which immediately preceded it. John had put the spotlight on human guilt, but Jesus focused his message much more on the good news of God's grace. That 'good news' lay at the heart of everything he was to say and do. He communicated his teaching in everyday stories of ordinary people in commonplace situations – but those seemingly simple parables were, in fact, invitations to see through the apparently mundane events of life to the mystery of a God whose essential nature is love and whose most apt name is Father.

His words and actions were all of a piece. He sought out the company of the marginalized and despised, offering them a forgiveness and acceptance they had never experienced before. Everything he did was a disclosure of the character of an infinitely loving God in a human life. His miracles were a demonstration of the hand of God in healing and providing for his children. And his death and resurrection were the ultimate revelation of the triumph of love over hate, good over evil, forgiveness over sin, life over death. In short, the Jesus we meet in the Gospels brings – indeed, he *is* – good news *about* God and good news *from* God.

The Greek word *euangelion* occurs more than seventy times in the New Testament and it's the word that's translated in English as 'good news'. Even the word 'gospel' that we use to sum up the Christian message is derived from the Anglo-Saxon words *god spel*, meaning 'good story'. The story of Jesus is good news – a good story – from beginning to end. It's not by accident that the first four books of the New Testament which tell the story of his ministry and witness to his identity as the Son of God are described as 'the four *Gospels*'. To speak of Jesus is to tell good news.

If being in the company of Jesus is the centre from which we move out in ever-widening circles, then right at the hub is good news, the best news the world can ever hear: *God is love and he reveals himself fully in Jesus.* To begin from any other point – however worthy our intentions, however passionate our desire to follow, however sound our theology in other respects, however morally right our actions, however deep our desire to serve humanity – is to miss the mark. We will fail to be true followers of Jesus and our efforts will count for little.

I've been fortunate enough to run the London Marathon half a dozen times. Only the elite runners get to line up right on the starting line. The rest of us less talented athletes form part of a crowd that stretches back for a very long way. The slower your predicted finishing time, the further back you are. You can be shuffling forwards for fifteen minutes before you even reach the starting line! But until you do, the race hasn't begun. And you can jog on the spot or jump up and down as much as you like, but they won't give you a medal for that. Once or twice I've glanced at some of my fellow runners just as we cross the line to start the race proper, only to discover that they look exhausted already. They've used up all their energy before the race has started. I think I've seen the same worn-out expression on the faces of some of my fellow believers who've still to discover that you don't even begin to follow Jesus until you cross the starting line and grasp the truth that it begins with the good news of the gospel, not with the hard graft of human effort.

Kingdom come

There's still more to this opening sortie in Jesus' campaign. The declaration of good news is linked with a promise for which the people of Israel had waited a long time: *The kingdom of God is near*. This is the consistent theme that runs through his teaching. It's like a recurring motif in a great musical composition. He refers to it again and again. He frequently gives imaginative pictures of what 'the kingdom' might be like in his parables. Biblical scholars constantly and rightly remind us that the phrase 'the kingdom of God' (or, as Matthew's Gospel has it, 'the kingdom of heaven') refers not to a *place* but to the *reign* or the *rule* of God. Wherever God's will is done, wherever his sovereign rule is obeyed, something of the kingdom of God can be seen.

Often, however, things don't look as if God is in control. Throughout her long and troubled history, the nation of Israel suffered at the hands of nations that were larger and more powerful politically and militarily. But despite her repeated failures to be the people God had called her to be, her faith in God remained alive. Across long centuries, the hope that God would break through and assert his just and wise rule sustained the people of Israel through their darkest days of defeat and exile. The people prayed for God's kingdom – his sovereign rule – to break through. And the prophets pointed to the Day of the Lord when God would put all wrongs right and his people would return to their homeland and be free once again.

The hope of God's coming kingdom went beyond their desire for national regeneration, however. It was the recognition deep in Israel's understanding of God's plan – often faint and

submerged, sometimes stronger and clearer – that the anticip-
ated breakthrough of God's rule was not just about Israel's
restoration but about the renewal of the entire creation, which
human sin and selfishness had twisted and corrupted. Israel's
purpose as God's chosen people was to declare and live out the
truth of God's rule. They were to be a picture of what life
would look like when God is in control. They were to be his
servants in bringing the good news of God to a world that
was morally diseased and spiritually desperate. Sadly, Israel's
record in playing their part in establishing the kingdom of God
on earth was chequered, to say the least. Again and again
God had to discipline them as they strayed from his will and
were seduced by the pagan gods and the selfish goals of the
nations around them.

*But now, at last, here is Jesus announcing that the time has come:
the kingdom is here!* The long-awaited reign of God is now upon
us. And, more to the point, its imminent emergence is insepar-
ably bound up with his ministry. As his first disciples reflected
on his life and ministry they came to see that all he would do
and say from this point on would mean nothing less than the
inauguration of the loving and just rule of his Father. His
miracles and healings would be both works of compassion and
signs of the new order when all things would be made new
and whole. His death and resurrection would secure victory
over the rebellious and destructive powers of evil that have for
so long blighted God's good creation. His ascension would
guarantee his authority over all things with his Father. And his
promised appearing at the end of this present age would finally
bring his redemptive work to glorious completion.

About turn

To proclaim the arrival of the kingdom of God as Jesus did was
to leave his hearers with no room for uncommitted neutrality

or idle curiosity. This is not an interesting speculative concept whose merits are to be discussed at length, much as one might debate the relative merits of the latest fad in wall-art. It's much more like that iconic First World War poster issued by the British government in 1914. In recruiting offices all over the country the image of Lord Horatio Herbert Kitchener, the Secretary of State for War, stared into the eyes of the young men of Britain. No-one who has seen it – including those born long after the cessation of the conflict to which it relates – can ever forget it. Kitchener fixes you with a steely gaze, his finger points directly at you, and the caption seems almost to leap off the page: *Your country needs YOU*. This isn't a portrait to be examined dispassionately or appreciated artistically. This is a picture that challenges the viewer and demands a response. Many a young man left home and family, took the king's shilling, donned the uniform of the British Army and died in the trenches of France because of the challenge of that poster.

The kingdom of God, like the poster of Kitchener, demands a response. *Repent and believe the good news* is the challenge that Jesus makes. And we need to be clear what Jesus is calling for. Normally we speak of repentance purely in terms of turning away from our own sins and turning towards God for forgiveness. That's certainly part – and a vitally important part – of what Jesus is saying here, but it isn't the whole truth. The reason and incentive for our repentance is the coming of the kingdom of God, his righteous reign in which love and justice will hold sway. The call to repent is more than merely an invitation to forsake our sins and be forgiven. It's nothing less than a call to align our whole lives with the values of God's kingdom, to live in a radically different way, to devote ourselves to working for the kingdom, to play our part in bringing God's plan of redemption and renewal to fruition, and to make the service of others in Christ's name our overriding ambition. We are to be citizens of the kingdom. We are to be agents of transformation. We are to do the work of God's kingdom wherever we are and share its summons to commitment and action with everyone we encounter.

Centre point

To believe the good news will require so much more than simply giving mental assent to certain statements of faith and formulations of doctrine, important as they are. It will involve us in taking Jesus at his word. It will involve us in risking everything on the conviction that the good news he brings really is true, even when all the evidence seems to suggest the contrary. It will mean seeking to live like Jesus, in obedience to God and in service to others for the sake of the gospel. And it will mean our lives *actually becoming* good news by the way we embody and express the values of the kingdom. In short, it will mean, as someone so memorably expressed it, living in such a way that it doesn't make any sense unless there is a God.

Thomas R. Kelly, the American Quaker, confronts his readers in one of his books with a question that takes us to the heart of true discipleship:

> Ask yourself: Am I down in the flaming centre of God? Have I come into the deeps, where the soul meets with God and knows his love and power? Have I discovered God as a living Immediacy, a sweet Presence, and a stirring, life-renovating Power within me?[1]

That is the centre in which Jesus lived and from which he reached out to redeem a lost world. There's no better – indeed, there's no other – place in which we can be nourished and from which we can begin to follow him and share in the work of his kingdom.

Going Deeper

1. Back in the 1980s David Watson wrote these words:

> Christians in the West have largely neglected what it means
> to be a *disciple of Christ*. The vast majority of western
> Christians are church-members, pew-fillers, hymn-singers,
> sermon-tasters, Bible-readers, even born-again-believers
> or Spirit-filled-charismatics – but not true disciples of Jesus.
> If we were willing to learn the meaning of real discipleship
> and actually to become disciples, the church in the West
> would be transformed, and the resultant impact on
> society would be staggering.
>
> This is no idle claim. It happened in the first century . . .[2]

Are his criticisms of the church still valid in our time? And
– equally importantly – are they valid criticisms of you?

2. Mark Greene has identified two issues facing us today:

> First, our church communities need to become much more
> open, interactive, personal and expressive – easier places to
> come to, easier communities to belong to. Second, we need
> to return to Jesus' instruction to 'make disciples', to become
> life-long learners and practitioners in learning communities
> – communities that are focused on equipping people to go
> where those who don't know Jesus are.[3]

How seriously does your church community take those
challenges? And what can you, as part of that community,
do to help?

2. Crucifixion

Couldn't we do without the cross?

During Tony Blair's time as prime minister of the United Kingdom, his Christian faith was a constant source of concern to his advisors. Fearing that any open declaration of his beliefs might damage his standing with the voters, Alistair Campbell, his communications director, once famously and brusquely told an American reporter who dared to ask a question about the PM's religious convictions, 'We don't do God!' And for his entire term of office they worked hard to ensure that he lived by that dictum. One of the most anxious moments for his team of apprehensive minders came on a Good Friday. Blair was taking part in a procession of the cross between the Anglican and Roman Catholic churches in his Sedgefield constituency. An eager young PR aide was assigned to make sure that 'at all costs' his boss was not photographed anywhere near the cross. Blair agreed to keep a suitable distance between himself and the cross, and to walk at the back of the procession. But even this was not enough to allay the concerns of the young man from party headquarters. Without so much as a hint of irony he asked, 'Couldn't we have the procession without the cross?'[1]

Notwithstanding the failure of the over-eager party worker to grasp either the significance of Good Friday or the nature of the procession, his anxiety isn't difficult to understand. His job was to make sure that the prime minister looked confident and self-assured, a *winner* – the kind of man you can rely on in a crisis. The cross, it has to be admitted, sends out a very different message. We may have sanitized it by turning it into a piece of decorative art, or glamorized it by wearing it as an item of jewellery, but the reality of the cross in first-century Palestine was very different. It was the death penalty of choice for the Roman authorities. And they knew a thing or two about crushing rebellions and dealing with those individuals who were foolhardy enough to disrupt the *Pax Romana* that held their far-flung and disparate empire together.

Crucifixion was bloody, violent and public, and no-one who witnessed it would ever forget it. The unnatural position in which the body was made to hang hindered circulation and resulted in a level of pain that was excruciating; the wounds of the nails, passing through the parts of the hands where the nerves and tendons are set, turned even the slightest attempted movement into the most intense torture; the wounds inflicted on the victim quickly became infested and inflamed in the heat and dust of the day, and a raging thirst would only add to this indescribable suffering; death, which often took days, would come as a welcome release.

Yet the cross, one of the worst instruments of torture ever devised by humankind, stands at the heart of the gospel. It is the iconic symbol of the Christian faith and the inescapable reminder of the manner in which its founder died. Only our familiarity with the story prevents us from fully realizing just how utterly astonishing a creed with a cross at its centre really is. Imagine your reaction to a religion whose emblem was the electric chair or the hangman's noose! And here's the really surprising thing about the way in which the New Testament speaks about the cross: *neither Jesus himself nor the writers of the Gospels view it primarily as a travesty of justice or a tragic mishap.* On the contrary, they celebrate it. The consistent witness of the New Testament is that the cross is central both to the working out of God's will for the redemption of the world and to the fulfilment of the purpose of Jesus' mission.

There's a pivotal point in the Gospels where Jesus takes his disciples on retreat to Caesarea Philippi. He quizzes them as to what the popular verdict on him is. Then he poses the question in a more direct and personal form: 'But what about you?' he asks. 'Who do you say I am?' (Mark 8:29). It's Peter, of course, who makes his great confession that Jesus is the Messiah come from God. But that moment of faith-filled insight is immediately followed by what must have been to the disciples the most unexpected and unwelcome revelation – one that Jesus would repeat often in the days that followed: 'He then began to teach them that the Son of Man must suffer many things and be rejected by the elders, chief priests and teachers of the law, and that he must be killed and after three days rise again' (Mark 8:31). So convinced is he that this must be the route he takes, that Peter's attempts to dissuade him from this course bring one of the strongest rebukes that ever came from the lips of Jesus (Mark 8:32–33). Clearly we cannot eliminate the cross from the Gospel record without changing the story completely. But it raises the unavoidable question: Why did Jesus have to die?

Why did Jesus have to die?

History is replete with the stories of characters whose untimely deaths were the result of some kind of deep-seated death wish. In the case of Jesus, however, all the evidence indicates that he was certainly not a man possessed by a martyr complex. On the contrary, it points to the fact that he loved life and lived it to the full. Just think of the things he said and did.

He told *parables* – teasing tales based on the most acute observations of the natural world and everyday life. But they also pointed to the deepest spiritual realities. For Jesus, the great eternal truths of his Father's kingdom were revealed *in and through* the soil on which he walked, the seasons through which he lived and the simple events he observed going on all around him. Only a man with a zest for life and a delight in what others might dismiss as the minutiae of the here and now could have made such acute observations and told such provocative tales.

He loved *people* – all kinds of people. A seemingly promiscuous woman by a well in the midday sun, a respected member of the Jewish ruling council in the darkness of the midnight hour, a lonely tax-collector hiding in the low branches of a tree, hard-working fishermen mending their nets by a lake, a group of noisy children that his disciples wanted to dismiss – he was constantly surrounded by people. There had to be something magnetic and positive about his personality to attract people like he did.

To the annoyance of the religious establishment, he enjoyed *parties*. It wasn't just that he *turned up* at parties. It was more that wherever he went and whatever was happening, he tended to *turn it into* a party! The wedding at Cana in Galilee was heading for a big anticlimax until he changed water into wine. The widow of Nain was on her way to bury her son until Jesus raised him from the dead and turned a funeral into a festivity. Bartimaeus was destined to be stuck by the roadside begging for the rest of his days until Jesus healed him and he set out to follow his healer to places he'd never seen or been to in his life. Even at his own farewell meal with his disciples on the night before he died Jesus passed the cup and shared the bread and established a fellowship meal that will be celebrated until the end of time. His critics, contrasting his lifestyle with the asceticism of John the Baptist, even accused him of being 'a glutton and a drunkard' (Matthew 11:18–19)! This is a man who enjoyed life to the full.

So why did this most healthy of human beings, the most life-affirming man who ever lived, come to willingly embrace the most terrible of deaths? The answer has to lie in the fact that he was also a man of *prayer*. There was a persistent rhythm to his life. Periods of intense work alternated with times of intentional withdrawal. The daily involvement with people was punctuated by deliberate interludes of retreat and reflection. He frequently withdrew to be alone in the presence of God. It was in these times of prayer that he must increas-ingly have discerned what he must also have dreaded most – that his ministry was leading inevitably to the cross. The struggle is played out in his prayer in Gethsemane on the eve of his trial. The cross is the last thing on earth he wants to go through. But, in the end, his desire for life is sacrificed to and sublimated in his determination to do his Father's will above everything else:

He fell with his face to the ground and prayed, 'My Father, if it is possible, may this cup be taken from me. Yet not as I will, but as you will.'

... He went away a second time and prayed, 'My Father, if it is not possible for this cup to be taken away unless I drink it, may your will be done.' (Matthew 26:39, 42)

What's the purpose of the cross?

The cross amazes me. I know about the 'theories of the atonement', but what really gets to me is the fact that on the cross God identifies completely with humanity and with his creation. He pays the ultimate price of suffering with us and for us. That's what really gets to me. It's the cross that makes sense of everything in the end. And I can't talk about the cross without talking about the resurrection that followed. That gives me a hope when things are at their worst. That's what got me through when Ellen died.
(Peter)

As he prayed and reflected on the unfolding truth of the nature of God in his Hebrew Scriptures, Jesus must have discerned a purpose in the cross. It was something deeper and more mysterious than the scheming of the high priest and his collaborating and compromised cronies in Jerusalem. It was something more powerful than the might of imperial Rome and its intolerance of any would-be Messiah. It was something more intentional than the fickle and easily manipulated mob who screamed, 'Crucify him!' In truth – and every page of the New Testament witnesses to this – the purpose of the cross was nothing less than the forgiveness of every wrong that has ever been done, the reconciliation of sinful human beings to a holy God and to each other, the restoration of God's image in humanity, and ultimately the renewal of the entire creation that has been marred and corrupted by sin. Jesus' executioners intended the cross to be the extinction of one troublesome human life. Instead, it brought about the emancipation of the whole troubled human race, and indeed the restoration of the whole of creation.

When we think about the cross, we're in the presence of the unfathomable miracle of divine love. The depth of its meaning is beyond the confines of our finite comprehension and our limited vocabulary. Sometimes (like Peter, in the comment above) we refer to the various ways in which the New Testament writers speak of the death of Jesus as 'theories of the atonement'. But it's much more helpful to view these insights into the cross as powerful and imaginative word pictures rather than as abstract theological concepts. Their intention goes beyond helping us to *understand* the cross intellectually. Their primary purpose is to enable us to *appropriate* the work of the cross by grasping it imaginatively, emotionally and spiritually.

The cross is like a many-faceted jewel whose various surfaces reflect the light in different ways according to the angle from which it is viewed. When theologians speak of *penal substitution* they are giving expression to one of the central truths of the gospel: we all stand before a holy God as unworthy sinners. If God were only a God of justice, humanity could expect nothing other than punishment. But he's a God of infinite love who sent Jesus to be the world's Saviour. And on the cross Jesus dies for us, carrying our sins and bearing the penalty that we deserve. But there are additional ways of looking at the meaning of the cross. So the death of Jesus is often described as the *perfect sacrifice*. We're being reminded of the Old Testament ritual of sacrifice in which the blood of the animal would be sprinkled over the assembled worshippers as a sign of their cleansing from the moral stain of their sin. And we're being invited to see that the death of Jesus on the cross – his life offered in perfect obedience to his Father – makes us clean and new in the eyes of God. Or, when the cross is equated with a *ransom* paid for us, the reality being set before us is that Jesus, by his willing death, sets us free from slavery to sin by doing for us what we could never do for ourselves and by doing so at the cost of his own life. Or we can come at it from yet another perspective. We live in a world in which it's so easy to feel that we're simply at the mercy of evil forces before which we stand helpless. So the New Testament writers encourage us by graphically depicting the cross as the *great victory* of infinite goodness and perfect love over all the powers of darkness and evil. None of these pictures is the whole truth, and they are not mutually exclusive. The meaning and power of the cross is bigger than all of them. What you see depends on where you stand. The truth that shines on us depends on the question we are asking.

The cross of Jesus is the inevitable manifestation of the destructiveness of evil. It is also the ultimate demonstration of God's transforming, forgiving love. Here, as nowhere else, we face the depravity of evil and human sinfulness. The only perfectly good man who ever lived is pinned to a cross on trumped-up charges after an unfair trial at the hands of corrupt officials. No amount of well-meaning sentiment can change those facts. But in offering his life in obedience to his Father, in loving and forgiving in the face of such malevolence, Jesus overcomes evil with the extravagant grace and goodness of God. His death changes everything for ever. He transforms an instrument of execution into the means of our salvation.

Why are we called to carry the cross?

Over a period I'd grown more and more fascinated by Jesus and more attracted to him. I knew in my heart that I wanted to follow his way. It made sense at a level deeper than I could explain. But it just seemed too costly. I had plans and a career and everybody told me that I had a big future ahead of me. And I knew that a whole lot of things would have to change and that some things might have to go completely if I went all the way with this Jesus thing. All I could think was, 'It'll be like dying to give all that up.'

And, in the end, that's exactly what it was like – a kind of dying. It was painful and I struggled over it for months but in the end I just gave in. It was peaceful and oddly liberating to let go of all that stuff. And I think I had a real sense of direction for the first time in my life. I guess that's what it means to take up your cross and follow Jesus. That's certainly how it was for me.

(Megan)

If Peter and the other disciples were disturbed by the fact that their Master must take the way of crucifixion, they were not allowed to dwell exclusively on that unpalatable thought for too long. No sooner had Jesus alerted them to the manner of his own impending death, than he turned to everyone within hearing with words that must have shocked them to the core. The followers of Jesus must take the same pathway as their Master! 'Then he called the crowd to him along with his disciples and said: "If anyone would come after me, he must deny himself and take up his cross and follow me"' (Mark 8:34). If there were any first-century equivalents of Tony Blair's spin-doctors among Jesus' inner circle of disciples, they must have been experiencing something close to apoplexy! You can almost hear their objections: *This is no way to gather committed supporters or to kick-start a movement. Surely there needs to be some kind of 'win' for anyone enlisting in the cause – something to sweeten the pill and soften the blow? The message needs to be more upbeat, not this sombre doom-and-gloom stuff!* But that kind of reaction fails to come to terms with the radical nature of discipleship and the topsy-turvy teaching of Jesus. He constantly overturns the cold logic of human reasoning and replaces it with the red-hot love of God's all-consuming grace.

No deals

The stark nature of Jesus' call leaves no room for ambiguity. If you want to be a follower, then you do it on his terms. You don't negotiate a deal, you make a decision. Discipleship isn't an attractive career choice to be selected from a variety of competing alternatives. It's an absolute commitment to a lifelong journey from which there must be no turning back. Put like that it may sound harsh, but everyone knows that the really important choices in life are like that. There comes a point at which the cogitating and the bargaining have to stop and you simply have to make up your mind.

Some years ago I went on an outward-bound course with a group of teens and twenty-somethings. I was keeping up with them and tackling all the challenges they were up for, until the instructor led us to a point about 5 metres above a river and invited us to jump into the water below. Without a moment's hesitation, everyone leapt off the bank – everyone, that is, except me. I stood there, paralysed by my lifelong fear of jumping from any kind of height. But in the end, with some encouraging words from the instructor ringing in my ears, I shut my eyes very tight, prayed very hard, and jumped. To my utter amazement and enormous relief, I lived to tell the tale.

As we walked back to the lodge together, the instructor went on to tell me of his own experience when he was interviewed for the job. After twenty minutes of questions, one of the interviewing panel took him outdoors to a point by the river's edge much higher than the one I'd just jumped from. Then he turned to the somewhat puzzled interviewee and said, 'I'm going to jump into the river. I want you to do it too. So either jump or don't. I'm not going to try to persuade you.' And with that he dived into the river.

'So what did you do?' I asked my instructor.

'I jumped,' he replied. 'And that's why they offered me the job. Not because I gave the right answers in reply to the questions, but because I was ready to respond to the challenge.'

I often tell that story when explaining the response that's needed to the call of Jesus. *There comes a point when you just have to make up your mind.*

No limits

No-one has ever sounded an appeal to commitment in more absolute terms than those in which Jesus couches the call to discipleship. Even in Christian circles, we all too often devalue the currency of his words. Self-denial has tended to become little more than a handy slogan for giving up something we enjoy for a limited period for the sake of a worthy cause. But that falls far short of what's meant here. Jesus isn't speaking of denying ourselves some pleasure or other. He's being much more radical than that. As William Barclay, the great Scottish Bible teacher, expressed it: 'To deny oneself means in every moment of life to say no to self and yes to God. To deny oneself means once, finally, and for all to dethrone self and to enthrone God.'[2]

When he followed that by inviting his hearers to 'take up [the] cross', Jesus put the cost of following him beyond any doubt. For his original audience it was a particularly vivid and daunting image. Before the actual moment of crucifixion, the Roman authorities took the opportunity to humiliate the convicted criminal and to give a terrible warning to the populace at large of the price of breaching the law. The victim would carry the cross-beam to the place of execution. When you saw such a sight you knew that you were watching a man on his way to his own funeral and to a bloody and terrible death.

We've often managed to minimize the impact of these words. It's commonplace to refer to some difficulty in our lives as 'the cross I have to bear'. That's not what Jesus meant. Taking up the cross isn't some awkward inconvenience. It's not even an unpleasant illness or a difficult circumstance. It's nothing less than the willingness to sacrifice everything – *everything* – for the sake of the gospel. Taking up the cross means that no price is so great and no pain is so severe that they will keep us from following the One who paid the ultimate price and suffered the most agonizing pain for us.

No loss

However, if all this makes discipleship sound negative and doom-laden, that's only because we've still to reckon with the words that follow: 'For whoever wants to save his life will lose it, but whoever loses his life for me and for the gospel will save it' (Mark 8:35). That same paradox which is at play in the death of Jesus – *his sacrificial death releases a greater life and a larger love that reaches and redeems humanity* – is also at work in the experience of every one of his followers. We're called to walk the way of the cross and to die to self only so that we can discover life in all its fullness. To hold on to life as we know it is to miss the opportunity to experience life as it should be – in all its fullness. Followers of Jesus give up all claims to self in order to be *truly themselves* by the transforming power of God. The self-centredness that stubbornly inhabits the centre of our being will ultimately destroy us unless it's driven out and replaced by a God-centredness that's truly liberating. As Jim Elliot, the martyred missionary to the Auca Indians, so memorably put it: 'He is no fool who gives up what he cannot keep for what he cannot lose.'

The bottom line is that there is no discipleship without death to self-centred living. You can't follow Jesus without breaking free from narrow self-interest. You can't find liberty without losing your life for his sake and for the sake of the good news he brings and that the world needs to hear. It's undeniably a tough bargain to strike, but everyone who has ever made it will stake their lives that it is the best investment they ever made.

Going Deeper

1. Count Nicholas Ludwig von Zinzendorf was born into one of Europe's most wealthy and noble families in 1700. As a young man he wrestled with the decision as to which direction his life should take. During a visit to the art gallery in Düsseldorf he saw Domenico Feti's painting *Ecce Homo*, 'Behold the Man', in which the artist depicted Jesus wearing the crown of thorns. Underneath the painting was the caption: 'This have I done for you. Now what will you do for me?' That moment changed him for ever. Taking Jesus seriously had to mean more than believing the truth about him or even trusting him for forgiveness. Von Zinzendorf became a passionate and committed disciple.

   Take some time to think about the cross. It might be helpful to look at a painting of the Calvary scene by one of the great artists. How does the image of Jesus on the cross challenge your life?

2. Arthur Blessitt has walked 38,000 miles in 38 years – carrying a large wooden cross. He has been arrested or imprisoned over twenty times, stoned, assaulted, stuck in war zones and military coups, and has faced a guerrilla firing squad in Nicaragua. He has been run over three times, the cross has been stolen and he has dropped it in the sea. He has also scaled mountains with it, including Mount Fuji.

He says he has been mostly welcomed by churches, 'if they knew what I was doing', although some were less friendly. 'When you're totally unknown, there's a lot of scepticism, and if you need to leave the cross at a church, "park it", people would ask: "What denomination are you?" There was often a real interrogation, which you never found if you wanted to leave it at a bar or night-club.'

He calls the cross 'a conversation-opener, not a barrier', and he 'converses rather than preaches'. 'I share Christ in a pleasant way. I share what he was, and tell them he loves them. When you're on the road there are no barriers, when you're on the roadside you're in the pulpit.'[3]

Arthur Blessitt has found a way to take the cross into the lives of ordinary people and to make it a topic of conversation. How can we 'carry the cross' in a manner that attracts and does not repel people? How can we talk about the cross so that we too 'share Christ in a pleasant way'?

3. The following books might be helpful for discovering more about what Christians believe the death of Jesus has accomplished. *Cross-Examined* by Mark Meynall (new edition, 2010) is a short, accessible read. *The Cross of Christ*, a classic by John Stott (new edition 2006), and *The Message of the Cross* by Derek Tidball (2001) both provide more in-depth study. All three are published by IVP.

3. Imitation

These days you can walk into any Christian bookshop and find a bewildering array of English translations of the Bible. It wasn't always like this. As recently as fifty years ago, the only access most English speakers had to the words of Scripture was the magnificent but archaic language of the Authorized (or King James) Version published in the reign of James I of England more than three centuries earlier. It's hardly surprising, then, that in the mid-1950s the appearance of new translations was greeted with some enthusiasm by those who wanted to read and understand the Bible in the language of the day. In response to such interest the BBC recorded a radio interview on 3 December 1953 with two very different men who had recently produced their own translations of the four Gospels. One of those men was the formidable E. V. Rieu, a classical scholar of some distinction.

Rieu was known and respected as the editor of the Penguin Classics and as an articulate and eloquent translator of the works of Homer. He had undertaken a translation of the four Gospels at the request of his publishers, who saw a gap in the market for a version aimed more at interested sceptics than committed believers. As an academic, he told the interviewer, he had approached his task in an enquiring and scholarly manner. But he went on to explain that it was his son who had made two perceptive comments about his father's encounter with the stories of the life and teaching of Jesus: 'It will be very interesting to see what Father makes of the Gospels,' he said. And then he added, 'It'll be still more interesting to see what the Gospels make of Father.' For anyone who is serious about following Jesus, these remain significant questions. What do we make of the Gospel records? And what will they make of us?

What do we make of the Gospels?

It's difficult, even impossible, to slot the four Gospels into some generally recognized literary category. Taken together, they're the primary source of our knowledge of the life of Jesus – but they're unlike any modern biography. They never describe what Jesus looked like and they never try to analyse his personality. Mark and John tell us nothing at all about his birth or his background. On the other hand, the amount of space all four Gospels devote to his death and the events of the last few days of his life would seem disproportionate to any modern biographer. There's evidence to suggest that much of what they record is based on eyewitness accounts of events, but Matthew and Luke seem to have borrowed much of their material from Mark. And John writes in a style and from a perspective that's very different from the other three Gospel writers. It's all very confusing! Clearly this is a genre unlike any other.

So what can we make of it? Scholars have noticed that the Gospels are made up largely of short accounts of specific incidents. Often they're accounts of Jesus' encounters with a variety of individuals or with groups of people like the Pharisees. Sometimes they highlight his power over disease or evil or natural forces. At other times they culminate in one of his memorable sayings. Occasionally, when the Gospel writers report the same incident, there are variations in detail which seem to suggest that they were concerned to draw out different aspects of the incident they're relating.

Several conclusions emerge from all this scrutiny. In the first place, despite the scepticism of a minority of scholars, the Gospels stand up well to close investigation. There's no convincing reason to think that they're merely the product of some overactive, pious imagination. They give every impression of being built on a firm bedrock of historical fact. At the same time it's clear that they don't set out to be 'objective' in the sense that a twenty-first-century historian or newspaper reporter would understand that word. They relate the story of Jesus from the definite standpoint of committed faith in the truth of his identity as the Son of God, and with the explicit purpose of calling their readers to that same faith. Academic investigation of the Gospels is both legitimate and necessary. Truth that will not stand the enquiry of honest scholarship is no truth at all. But to stop at that is to miss the point completely. As E. V. Rieu's son so rightly said, the real point is not what we make of the Gospels, but what they make of us.

There's something about reading the Gospels that's different from anything else I've ever read. It's not just the sense you get that they have a ring of truth about them. I mean, you just couldn't and wouldn't make up a story like that. Even some of the main characters like Peter and the other disciples often come out of it looking more like zeros than heroes. It's got to be true! But what really gets me is the way the stories draw you in, make you feel like you're really there, one of the crowd watching. I read a lot and I don't know any other kind of writing or reporting that has quite this effect on me.
(James)

What do the Gospels make of us?

Facts

The most obvious thing to say about the Gospels is that they *provide us with the facts* about Jesus. And, contrary to what the devotees of some popular current spiritualities will tell you, facts are important. No sensible person buys a house or a car – or anything else for that matter – without finding out some basic information about the product they're considering purchasing. No sensible person, however much in love they might feel, gets married without getting to know the person with whom they intend spending the rest of their lives. And no sensible person commits to a religious faith without learn-ing as much as they can about the founder and the tenets of that faith.

The question is: *How much do you need to know about Jesus in order to make an intelligent and lasting commitment to him?* It was to answer that very question for a Roman official by the name of Theophilus that Luke set himself the task of writing his account of the life and ministry of Jesus. As he explains in the opening sentences of his Gospel:

Many have undertaken to draw up an account of the things that
have been fulfilled among us, just as they were handed down to
us by those who from the first were eye-witnesses and servants
of the word. Therefore, since I myself have carefully investigated
everything from the beginning, it seemed good also to me to
write an orderly account for you, most excellent Theophilus,
so that you may know the certainty of the things you have been
taught.   (Luke 1:1–4)

Clearly Luke and his fellow Gospel-writers believed that it was
not helpful or healthy to expect anyone to follow Jesus without
some knowledge of the facts about his life and teaching.

Faith
The Gospel writers were not, however, merely historians. They
wanted to do more than simply leave a reliable record of events
surrounding the life of an itinerant rabbi in first-century
Palestine. What they were really anxious to do was to *awaken
faith* in everyone who hears about Jesus. They were certain that
his life could not be explained exclusively in human and historical terms. They believed that in this one human life – indeed,
the only perfect and fully human life ever lived – they had seen
God in all his fullness. More than that, as they reflected on all
that had happened, they were convinced that through the death
of Jesus they had been reconciled to God, that he had been
raised to life on the third day, that he had poured out God's Spirit
on the church, and that he would one day come again as Lord
and Judge of humanity.

   When you believe that, you really want to share it with others
in such a way that they too will come to believe and to know
the new kind of life that Jesus has made possible by his life,
death and resurrection. You can't tell them everything about
Jesus, but you can tell them enough, especially the things that

will inspire them to believe in him. And that's exactly what John says he is doing towards the end of his Gospel: 'Jesus did many other miraculous signs in the presence of his disciples, which are not recorded in this book. But these are written that you may believe that Jesus is the Christ, the Son of God, and that by believing you may have life in his name' (John 20:30–31).

Following

I was just a kid when I heard a preacher say that we should always tell people who were not yet Christians that they shouldn't look at our lives because we're so imperfect. Instead, he insisted, we should encourage them to 'fix their eyes on the Master', to look only at Jesus. I was no child prodigy when it came to theology, but I knew immediately there was a flaw somewhere in his reasoning. Within minutes I'd worked it out: *I couldn't see Jesus!* And I was taken to church every Sunday and several times in the week for good measure. So what hope was there, I wondered, for most of the other kids in my class at school and their parents who never went to church? They had to see Jesus in the way *we* lived. If they couldn't see a good model of his life in the lives of his followers, then they were well and truly stuck.

I have to say that I think I was smarter than that preacher. In fact, I've become convinced that the ultimate purpose of the Gospels goes beyond just producing believers who are well clued up on the facts of their faith. It's to *create followers*, men and women who will model their lives on Jesus and who will seek to demonstrate his kind of joyful and extravagant love in their lives.

The *information* provided in the Gospels which gives us the facts about Jesus is good. And the *inspiration* of the Gospels which awakens faith in our hearts is even better. But unless it leads to *imitation* – modelling our lives on him and becoming more and more like him – the process is incomplete. That's essentially how the good news of Jesus is shared. Of course, we're all imperfect, we're all 'a work in progress', but there's no escaping the fact that followers of Jesus are called to live in such a way that others are attracted by their lives. That becomes clearer than ever if we understand the culture in which Jesus first called his disciples.

It's more than twenty years since I first went to Miss Jardine for piano lessons. I was just a kid, about twelve at the time, but I've never forgotten those evenings. She was always respectful – even to a twelve-year-old kid. But she never let you away with anything. She sussed you out fast if you hadn't done your practice that week. And she really knew how to teach. She'd play a couple of lines of the music – the tricky bits – nice and slow. Then she'd get me to do the same. Sometimes we repeated the process half a dozen times, but she never seemed to despair of me making some progress. And here's the thing I remember most. Sometimes when she played she'd ask me to put my hands on top of hers. 'Feel how I'm playing it,' she'd say. Then I'd try to play it with the same feeling. It's uncanny how that seemed to work! I'll always be a limited kind of pianist, but she got me to play way beyond my abilities. I often tell young people about her when I'm trying to explain how I think we learn to be disciples of Jesus.
(Alice)

Becoming a disciple

Going to school
Formal instruction for Jewish boys in Jesus' day usually began at around four or five years of age in the local synagogue, where

they would be schooled in the Torah, the first five books of the Bible. By the time they reached the age of ten they were deemed ready to be tutored in the oral traditions arising from the reflections of generations of scholars on the written Scriptures. Great emphasis was given to memorizing long passages and by the age of thirteen many of these students could recite the entire Torah from memory. Then, having been thoroughly grounded in the teaching of the Hebrew Scriptures, most young men would learn a trade and begin to play their part in supporting their families. But the more gifted would continue for another couple of years. Alongside learning the practical skills needed for their working lives, they would study other parts of the Hebrew scriptures such as the writings of the great prophets.

Finding a rabbi

By the age of fifteen, formal education would be at an end for everyone except a very select group. They were an elite band – the best of the best – who would seek to continue their education to an advanced level by applying to a rabbi. 'Rabbi', which derives from a Hebrew word meaning 'great' or 'revered', was a deferential title given to men who were recognized as teachers of the Jewish faith. Such men were revered for their understanding and interpretation of Scripture and their teaching was authoritative in all matters of life and religion. They would carefully question any young men who applied to them, and would accept them only when satisfied as to their aptitude and dedication.

Being a disciple

It was at the point of being accepted as a disciple of a rabbi that the life of the eager young applicant would change for ever. It wasn't simply that, like many young people going off to university today, they would leave home and family for the first time. This certainly wasn't a case of attending lectures every day and handing in a couple of essays every month. And nothing could have been further removed from the stereotypical student life of today with its combination of late-night parties, too much booze, handing in essays at the last minute and getting up each day at the crack of noon! The whole point of becoming a disciple was not just to learn more stuff in order to add a couple of letters after your name and get a better job. It was a much bigger deal than that.

The disciple's whole aim was to *follow* his rabbi – literally and metaphorically. Throughout each day he would walk behind him, listening to his every word, watching his every move, absorbing his teaching and modelling his life on that of his rabbi. They even had a maxim to encourage attentive disciples to stay up close and personal with their teacher: 'Cover yourself in the dust of your rabbi's feet.' The goal of every disciple was to become like his rabbi and to reach the place where he, too, would be a rabbi with disciples of his own. In fact, the Hebrew word for disciple – *talmid* – is much closer to the idea of being an apprentice than a student. It's intensely practical, not merely academic. It's about learning how to be and do, rather than simply mastering facts and gathering information. This was not instruction to enable you to pass an examination; this was not even education to equip you for employment; this was *an apprenticeship for living.*

Becoming like Jesus

To anyone who saw Jesus walking the dusty roads of Galilee with his disciples, he would have looked just like any other rabbi as he taught them and interacted with them. But there were some very significant differences between Jesus and the other teachers of his day. He didn't wait for Peter, James, John and the others to apply to him. Instead, he called them. *He took the initiative and chose them.* What's more, they were ordinary men, working at a trade. They weren't part of the scholarly elite, and they didn't belong to the brightest and best. They would have completed their formal studies in their teens. Now their lives were devoted to earning a living and providing for their families rather than learning the minutiae of the Law and the Prophets.

The most significant thing of all – the breathtaking thing – is that, in calling them to follow him as his disciples, he was paying them the ultimate compliment. In a culture in which discipleship was all about becoming like your rabbi, Jesus was saying to them, in effect, 'I believe that you can become like me.' The Son of God was calling them to learn from him and model their lives on his, so that one day they too would call others and become models of Christ-likeness for them to follow. Here's something to note: in the New Testament the word 'Christian' occurs only three times, but throughout the four Gospels and the story of the early church in Acts, the word 'disciple' is used more than 250 times. And it isn't just applied to the original twelve apostles. It's the characteristic description of *every* follower of Jesus. *We're all called to be disciples.*

It might be tempting to imagine that this principle of imitation was just an aspect of Jewish religious culture at the time of Jesus, but that's not the case at all. Imitation lies at the very heart of discipleship. It's also the key to sharing the Gospel effectively with others. Some twenty years after the death and resurrection of Jesus, the apostle Paul wrote a letter to the church in Thessalonica, a bustling seaport in Macedonia. It was a church he himself had planted and there's evidence to suggest that this young congregation was made up largely of Gentiles – non-Jews (Acts 17:4). But right here in this cosmopolitan city, a very different environment from the rural surroundings and dusty roads of Palestine, Paul highlights the same principle of imitation. He refers to his own lifestyle and its impact on the Thessalonians:

> We always thank God for all of you, mentioning you in our prayers . . .
>
> For we know, brothers loved by God, that he has chosen you, because our gospel came to you not simply with words, but also with power, with the Holy Spirit and with deep conviction. *You know how we lived among you for your sake. You became imitators of us and of the Lord . . .*   (1 Thessalonians 1:2–6, italics mine)

At first glance it sounds like arrogance: by imitating us, Paul insists, you imitated the Lord himself! But it is simply the principle of imitation and the practice of discipleship being played out. Paul modelled his life on that of Jesus. So inevitably, when others patterned their behaviour on what they saw in his life, they were becoming imitators of Jesus. The process doesn't stop there, however: ' . . . in spite of severe suffering, you welcomed the message with the joy given by the Holy Spirit. And so *you became a model to all the believers* in Macedonia and Achaia' (1 Thessalonians 1:6–7, italics mine). Paul discipled the Thessalonian believers and their lives, in turn, became the model for others. The disciples became the disciplers, the learners became the teachers, the imitators were imitated. And so the process continued.

Displaying the likeness

The other translator of the Gospels who took part in the BBC interview we referred to at the start of this chapter was J. B. Phillips, an Anglican vicar. He told how his efforts at translating the Bible into contemporary English had been stimulated by his experience of working with young people in London during the Second World War. One particular episode had imprinted itself on his mind. During the blackout, as the German bombers droned overhead, he had attempted to occupy a group of teenagers by reading to them from the Bible – the Authorized Version with its seventeenth-century English. Not surprisingly, he confessed, 'they couldn't make any sense of it at all'. So, 'in a very small and amateur sort of way', he began first to translate some of the New Testament letters. Then he moved on to the Gospels. His work might have gone no further than his youthful flock, but for the fact that he decided to send a copy of his efforts to one of his heroes, C. S. Lewis. The writer of the Narnia stories was greatly impressed and wrote back saying, 'It's like seeing an old picture that's been cleaned. Why don't you go on and do the lot?' Which is exactly what Phillips did, producing a translation that shed a whole new light on the Bible for many in his generation.

For most people in Britain today the story of Jesus is like an old, half-forgotten, dusty picture. We may not literally translate the Scriptures like J. B. Phillips or E. V. Rieu, but, as has often been said, our lives may well be the only Bible that the people around us will read. Even more importantly, our lives may well be the only glimpse of Jesus they will ever see. The challenge is for us to live in such a way that our lives clear away the confusion that distorts and discolours the picture of Jesus that so many people carry with them. The more accurately our lives model his, the greater will be the likelihood that they will see Jesus in us and discover him for themselves.

James Butler Bonham was one of the heroes who died in the defence of the Alamo in San Antonio, Texas, in 1836. Despite his honoured place in American history, there is no known portrait of the man. But the 2.5 million visitors to the Alamo each year leave the site with a clear image of Bonham in their minds. For, as they pass through the main entrance, their eyes are drawn to a painting of an impressive military figure with the following inscription:

> James Butler Bonham – no picture of him exists. This portrait is of his nephew, Major James Bonham, deceased, who greatly resembled his uncle. It is placed here by the family that people may know the appearance of the man who died for freedom.

The life of every follower of Jesus should serve a similar purpose to the portrait of James Butler Bonham's nephew. We're called to live in such a way that others will see in us and discover for themselves the liberating and life-transforming truth of the man who died to set us free and who still calls men and women to be his disciples.

Going Deeper

1. Read Mark 1:16–20. Read it aloud several times and try to visualize the scene in your mind. Imagine the thoughts and feelings of the first disciples. Now read it again. But this time imagine that Jesus turned up at your workplace or college, or while you were having a drink with some mates or a coffee at Starbucks. How would you feel and what would you do?

2. Who are the followers of Jesus who've had an impact on your life? What were the qualities that you admired in them? Which of those qualities would you want to imitate in your own life?

3. Thomas à Kempis was a fifteenth-century monk. His counsel to his fellow monks, which has been recorded in what we now know as *The Imitation of Christ*, includes these words:

> Christ urges us to mould our lives and characters in the image of his, if we wish to be truly enlightened and freed

from all blindness of heart. Let us therefore see that we endeavour beyond all else to meditate on the life of Jesus Christ . . .

Anyone who wishes to understand and to savour the words of Christ to the full must try to make his whole life conform to the pattern of Christ's life . . .

What good can it do you to discuss the mystery of God the Trinity in learned terms if you lack humility and so displease God? Learned arguments do not make a man holy and righteous, whereas a good life makes him dear to God.[1]

What would have to change in your life today if you seriously began to 'try to make [your] whole life conform to the pattern of Christ's life'?

4. Incarnation

A great try

What does it mean to live like Jesus today? And how would our neighbours recognize an authentic disciple in the twenty-first century? Ed Dobson, the vice-president of Spiritual Formation at Cornerstone University in Grand Rapids, Michigan, decided he was really going to give it a try. He was going to live as much like Jesus as he could. The most difficult part of the challenge, he explained, was following the teaching of Jesus, especially the instruction to bless people who persecute you. 'My youngest son did two tours in Iraq, and on the last tour, a friend of his was killed in action . . . and I was overwhelmed with grief and also with anger for the people who had made the roadside bomb, planted it and detonated it,' he said. 'And then I finally realized I had to pray for them and bless them, which is very, very hard to do.'

He did permit himself the occasional drink on the basis that he felt there was sound scriptural warrant for such an indulgence: 'I would often go down to the bar, sit up at the counter, drink a beer and talk about God . . . Jesus was accused of being a glutton and a drunkard,' he said. But Dobson interpreted the call to live like Jesus rather more literally than most. Besides reading through the four Gospels every week, he grew a beard, ate only kosher food, and observed the Jewish Sabbath.[1] You've got to give him full marks for a great try!

A great hymn

Impressed as I am by Dobson's sincerity and determination to go the whole way, I am less certain about the beard, the kosher food and the Sabbath observance. If we take that kind of thinking to its logical conclusion, we may well find ourselves walking everywhere in sandals, speaking only in Aramaic, preaching from fishing boats, reading from scrolls by the light of oil lamps and wearing long white robes! We could do all that and be no closer to the spirit and teaching of Jesus than the scribes and Pharisees who were indifferent or even antagonistic to his message. What's more, far from offering the world an authentic picture of the Christ-like life, we would simply serve to confirm the suspicions in the minds of many that Christianity is an outdated way of life suitable only for those with a peculiar religious gene.

I only got to know Bill in his later years. He was physically frail, but still alert and interested in everything that was happening in my life.

He'd been through the war, though he never said too much about that.
It was only after he died that I found out he'd been something of a hero
and he'd had a number of commendations for bravery. He hadn't had
much in the way of a formal education and I guess you'd have to say
his Christian faith was simple and unsophisticated. But he always
prayed with me. And he knew how to pray! Every time I closed the door
and walked down the path after I'd visited him, I always had this really
strong sense that I'd been in the presence of Jesus. And it was interest-
ing, after he died, how many people said they felt the same whenever
they met him.
(Liam)

Something less clumsily literal and much more spiritually radical
is needed if we're to live like Jesus in a culture far removed from
that of first-century Palestine. But this isn't just a problem of the
twenty-first century. The New Testament letters were written
largely to address this very issue. How were the followers of
Jesus – an ever-increasing number of them *non-Jewish* – to live
like Jesus in Rome, Galatia, Corinth, Ephesus or Philippi? How
were they to relate to their fellow believers and fellow citizens
in a manner that would enable others to see the reality of the
life of Jesus in their lives? Could they enter into the life of their
communities in the transforming manner that Jesus had entered
into our world? In short, how were they to live *incarnationally*?

One of the most glorious passages in the New Testament
was written precisely to answer those questions. Paul wanted
to encourage the believers in the Roman colony of Philippi to
demonstrate their new life in Christ by the way they behaved
towards each other. His reasoning is plain enough. If you are a
follower of Jesus, then that must show itself in the quality of
your relationships:

> If you have any encouragement from being united with Christ,
> if any comfort from his love, if any fellowship with the Spirit, if
> any tenderness and compassion, then make my joy complete by
> being like-minded, having the same love, being one in spirit and
> purpose. Do nothing out of selfish ambition or vain conceit, but
> in humility consider others better than yourselves. Each of you
> should look not only to your own interests, but also to the
> interests of others. (Philippians 2:1–4)

Sound and practical advice. True disciples should be humble,
compassionate, caring. You can't argue with that and the
members of the Philippian church must have nodded in
agreement when Paul's words were read to them. But then he
takes it to another level. 'Your attitude', he says, 'should be the
same as that of Christ Jesus.' With that he moves from prose to
poetry; he shifts from giving *instruction* to contemplating the
miracle of the *incarnation* – God becoming a human being. He
doesn't just focus on the *fact* that God has come among us in
Jesus, incredible as that is. His attention is much more on the
manner of his life among us. Other religions told of gods who
came down to earth as conquering warriors or mighty
monarchs. Jesus is very different:

> Who, being in very nature God,
>   did not consider equality with God something to be grasped,
> but made himself nothing,
>   taking the very nature of a servant,
>   being made in human likeness.
> And being found in appearance as a man,
>   he humbled himself
>   and became obedient to death – even death on a cross!
> Therefore God exalted him to the highest place
>   and gave him the name that is above every name,

that at the name of Jesus every knee should bow,
 in heaven and on earth and under the earth,
and every tongue confess that Jesus Christ is Lord,
 to the glory of God the Father.
(Philippians 2:5–11)

It's a magnificent passage. Most biblical scholars are agreed
that it's probably a fragment of an early Christian hymn, sung
in praise of Jesus who shared our humanity and willingly
suffered death on the cross for us. But what makes it so remarkable in this context is this: Paul doesn't refer to it because of its
theological insight or its liturgical beauty. He's not at this
moment concerned to give his Philippian readers a lesson in
doctrine or to remind them of a great worship song. He quotes
it simply because he wants them to understand what it means
to model their lives on Jesus. *If you want to learn the art and
practice of imitation*, he is saying, *then you need to grasp the wonder
and the nature of the incarnation.*

*Since we moved to Manchester in 2000, most of what we thought
and believed about incarnation has been challenged, shaped and
changed. When our son Joel was born, we really became vulnerable
in the sense that as first-time parents we had little idea of how life
was about to change, little idea how to bring up a child and little
idea what that meant in a community which is considered to have
the highest level of child poverty in the country. Having spent five
years working as service providers in Openshaw – running kids'
clubs, toddler groups and youth work – we suddenly found ourselves
as service users, lining up like everyone else, waiting our turn to
accept whatever help was available. This, then, was a lesson in
becoming like our neighbours, sharing the uncertainty, fear and
excitement of this particular life experience. In those days we became*

a little more human, a little more broken, a little more connected to our community.
(Gary)

A great lesson

Since Paul invites the believers in Philippi – all of whom were inexperienced followers of Jesus and few of whom would have studied theology – to reflect on the miracle of the incarnation, then we too can respond to his invitation. We too can try to distil the essence of the wisdom he offers us. Here are four simple words that might help us unlock at least some of the riches of Paul's teaching.

Filled . . .

At first glance the opening line of this ancient Christian hymn seems to distance us from Jesus. We are merely human and he is, after all, 'in very nature God'. Of course, we're right to acknowledge the awesome truth of who he was and is. The earliest believers – and every generation of Christians since – came to the irresistible conclusion that, if you take Jesus seriously, you can't define him in merely human terms. When you try to say who Jesus is, you just have to talk about God. That's all the more remarkable when you remember that those first Christians were monotheistic Jews. Their religion had taught them, above everything else, that there is only one God and no-one else should ever be ranked alongside him. But that one God, they were convinced, had come among them in Jesus. That, indeed, is the very heart of the incarnation – God becoming one of us. Every follower of Jesus understands how Thomas felt in the presence of the risen Jesus. We too want to bow before him and acknowledge that he is Lord and God (John 20:24–29).

Nonetheless, the Gospels are just as definite about his humanity as they are about his divinity. Jesus was not God disguised as a human being. God was not pretending to be one of us. 'God was pleased', as Paul explains it to the believers in Colosse, 'to have all his fulness dwell in him [Jesus]' (Colossians 1:19). But that does not make Jesus less human than us. Quite the opposite. His openness and obedience to God mean that he is what all of us were meant to be: he shares our humanity, but without the distortion of sin and selfishness. *His life is, in truth, the perfect template for ours.* Equally importantly, the experience of his followers at Pentecost was that they had received the Holy Spirit – the same Spirit that perfectly filled Jesus and that raised him from the dead. Through the presence of the Spirit they too were empowered and equipped to begin to live like Jesus.

That's why Paul prefaced the great incarnation hymn with the words: 'If you have any encouragement from being united with Christ, if any comfort from his love, *if any fellowship with the Spirit* . . . ' (Philippians 2:1, italics mine). Jesus was the perfect man, perfectly human and perfectly filled with the Spirit of God. Those who have acknowledged him as their Lord and Master have been joined with him through faith and united with each other in fellowship. And it's all the work of the same Spirit. Of course, he was the one human being who was perfectly filled with the Spirit of God. We're all imperfect – a 'work in progress'. But that progress is both our privilege and our calling simply because *we, like Jesus, are filled with the Spirit of God as we open ourselves to his grace and dedicate our lives to his will.* We're certainly not his equals, but we can and must follow his example.

. . . and emptied

The words 'made himself nothing' translate a phrase in the original Greek which literally means 'emptied himself'. The Son of God 'emptied himself' – he gave up every privilege and all status and poured himself out for others. We can never fully understand all that's contained in that seemingly simple little phrase. Nor can we adequately express its meaning in words. But countless Christians have testified to the truth that their experience has mirrored his: what is true of Jesus in perfect measure is also true for every one of his followers in principle. *Being filled with the Spirit of God always goes hand in hand with being emptied of self.*

To live incarnationally means to live in such a way that we make God accessible and available to others by who we are and what we do. So, by definition, people who are concerned to preserve their own status or position will never be able to live incarnationally. They will be too full of self to be filled with the Spirit, too preoccupied with their own importance to make room for God. But those who know what it means to be emptied discover one of the most liberating paradoxes in the world: *we become most fully ourselves when we are most filled with the Spirit of God.*

The day is marked indelibly on my brain: 23 September, 1999. Not my wedding anniversary, baptism or child's birthday but the first day I came to Manchester. The call to relocate to Darkest England is a tough one, and I personally wouldn't budge without a fight. It was a grey, rainy day which had somehow gone from being a 'visit' with a friend to being a job interview for the role of EDEN team leader at Openshaw – a post for which I genuinely do not remember applying. As the only candidate . . . my sad attempts to express lethargy towards the project and my own personal incompetence were in vain and I left the Salvation Army headquarters with a job offer in my hand and a feeling that my entire future was ebbing away before my eyes. That was of course exactly what was happening.
(Gary)[2]

Service . . .

To follow the words of Paul's great incarnation hymn to their conclusion is to come face to face with the One who, though 'being in very nature God', took 'the form of a servant', as most translations render it in English. But the fact is that 'servant' is too weak a word here. The word Paul uses in Greek is *doulos*, which is most accurately translated not as 'servant' but as 'slave'. This is *service without limit*, service which gives up all rights, service which goes all the way to death on a cross, service which is willing to live and die for others. This is service which identifies with people, empathizes with their pain and suffering, and bears the penalty of their sin and disobedience. This is the kind of service which took Jesus to the cross. It is the kind of service to which every follower of Jesus is called.

David Livingstone embraced this paradox of willing slavery as his life's purpose. In 1853, at the end of an arduous journey into the heart of Africa, he wrote in his journal:

> I will place no value on anything I have or may possess,
> except in relation to the kingdom of Christ. If anything will
> advance the interests of that kingdom, it shall be given away
> or kept only as by giving or keeping of it I shall most promote
> the glory of him to whom I owe all my hopes in time and
> eternity.

It was that spirit of reckless, selfless daring that enabled him to combine the vocations of Christian missionary, anti-slavery campaigner and scientific researcher. And it was that spirit that made him a hero to an entire generation who recognized in his commitment to incarnational service to the African continent a picture of the Lord he sought to serve.

Livingstone's last expedition, searching for the source of the Nile and investigating the slave trade, culminated in his death in 1873. When Florence Nightingale wrote that 'God has taken away the greatest man of his generation', she not only expressed the gratitude of millions; she also acknowledged the nature of genuine greatness that his life had served to highlight. It is the same greatness that is perfectly demonstrated in the life and death of Jesus and joyously celebrated in the incarnation hymn of Philippians. It is *the greatness of complete obedience to God's will*. And it is the greatness that leads to one of the most glorious 'therefores' in the New Testament.

. . . *and success*

> *Therefore* God exalted him to the highest place
>   and gave him the name that is above every name,
> that at the name of Jesus every knee should bow,
>   in heaven and on earth and under the earth,
> and every tongue confess that Jesus Christ is Lord,
>   to the glory of God the Father.
> (Philippians 2:9–11, italics mine)

To those who stood around the cross on Good Friday, the death of Jesus must have seemed anything but success. They must have seen it as a terrible and dismal failure. That is sometimes – maybe even often – the way with that kind of selfless service. Living incarnationally is no guarantee of instant or easy victory. Jesus died in the agony of crucifixion. Livingstone died in the isolation of the African bush. Many unknown and unsung followers of Jesus have faced apparent failure. But to end there is to miss the great 'therefore' of Paul's incarnation hymn. For those who walk in the company of Jesus, who seek to follow his example of obedient service, who seek to give all they are for others, there are ultimately no losing battles. They live under the protective shadow of God's 'therefore'. Because they have done their part, God will do his. What they have had to leave unfinished God will complete. What they have done imperfectly God will bring to perfection.

That kind of living and dying releases the transforming power of the resurrection. God raised Jesus from the dead and raised him to the highest place. God used Livingstone's life and witness to disturb the conscience of Europe about her responsibilities to Africa. God works his purposes through the efforts of his humblest servants. And beyond this present age there is the promise of ultimate vindication. The same God who exalts the name and announces the Lordship of Jesus acknowledges the name and endorses the work of every faithful servant. Everything that is done in the service of his kingdom and for the sake of others will form a vital and integral part of his project to renew and redeem his entire creation. That, in the end, is the only success worthy of the name.

Going Deeper

1. In his account of the early years of the Eden Project in Manchester's Openshaw district, Gary Bishop tells of some graffiti that held more truth than the 'artist' realized:

> A worker in Fitton Hill, Oldham, once had 'Jesus lives 'ere' daubed on his front door by a local youth. Needless to say that graffiti didn't get cleaned off for quite a while! In a very real sense, that person is a visible representation of God to his community – whenever people look at him they are to be reminded of what God is like, and if they ever wonder what God is like they can look at God's people to get an idea. If the church is absent from the great expanses of darkness throughout Britain, then how will they ever encounter the light?[3]

Where are the places in which you are called to live incarnationally? What kind of picture of God do people see in you?

2. Is being a disciple of Jesus the greatest priority in your life? Are there things that need to be 'emptied' from your life in order to make space for God's Spirit to fill you? Are your goals and ambitions aspects of your discipleship, or do they pull in opposite directions?

3. Here is a prayer you may like to pray:

> Father,
> Fill my life with your Spirit
> That I may grow in the likeness of your Son.
> Let my thoughts, words and deeds be directed by your
>   Spirit.
> And, as I model my life after the pattern of Jesus,
> May my life serve as an example to others.
> Amen.

Growing in the
community of believers

5. A worshipping community

Church – who needs it?

My opponent in the radio debate was already at the studio when I arrived. He greeted me cordially and I immediately warmed to him. It was obvious that we shared a sense of humour and a conviction that following Jesus was the best decision we'd ever made. What we didn't share was our view on the importance of church. He felt so strongly about it that he'd flown over from Northern Ireland at his own expense, and two minutes into the recording he presented his argument. He was courteous but uncompromising: 'Yes, I'm a committed follower of Jesus, but I don't go to church any longer and I'll give you three reasons why – I don't want to, I don't have to, and I don't need to!'

Clearly this was a man for whom church had not been a positive experience. He spoke about the 'all-out war' of Sunday mornings in years gone by when he and his wife would rush around madly trying to get four kids fed, dressed and off to church in good time. He registered his annoyance at the hypocrisy of some of the people he used to meet then and his irritation with the regimented nature of what passed for liberating worship. And he insisted that much of the way in which we 'do church' is merely cultural and has little to do with what the Bible actually teaches. I had to confess that on more than a few occasions I'd shared his frustration.

For all that, I found myself in disagreement with my affable opponent. I could share his enthusiasm for meeting with a few friends for stimulating conversation, Bible study and prayer. Like him, I too love to walk in the hills on a sunny day in pleasant company – what he described as 'the Big Wide Canopy Church'. But good as those things are, they're not quite what the New Testament means by church. At most they're a part of something larger, something more costly, but ultimately much more rewarding than simply being with a few like-minded Christian companions.

If we want to be effective followers of Jesus, church isn't an optional extra. It's integral to what it means to be a disciple. And when people talk about 'going to church' or 'not going to church', they're really missing the point. That makes it sound like something that's just a matter of personal taste – like going to the theatre. But church isn't, in the first instance, a *place* to which we decide to go or not to go. Rather, it's a *body* to which we belong, a living organism of which we need to be a part if we are to experience the full and genuine life of a follower of Jesus.

The new community

The first time the gospel was preached on the day of Pentecost, Peter's sermon was so powerful that some three thousand people became believers and were baptized. *Then they became part of the church*, sharing in the life and worship of a new and exciting community. Luke paints a vibrant picture of what that community was like in his story of the earliest church:

> They devoted themselves to the apostles' teaching and to the fellowship, to the breaking of bread and to prayer. Everyone was filled with awe, and many wonders and miraculous signs were done by the apostles. All the believers were together and had everything in common. Selling their possessions and goods, they gave to anyone as he had need. Every day they continued to meet together in the temple courts. They broke bread in their homes and ate together with glad and sincere hearts, praising God and enjoying the favour of all the people. And the Lord added to their number daily those who were being saved.
> (Acts 2:42–47)

Whatever was happening as they met together for the breaking of bread, for prayer and for teaching was so powerful and life-transforming that it spilled over into their everyday lives. It caused them to care and share in a way that was radically different from anything they'd done before – and that has been the blueprint for Christian living throughout history.

Justin Martyr lived in the second century AD and became a follower of Jesus after searching for truth in the philosophical systems of his day. In a letter to the Roman emperor Antoninus Pius defending the beliefs and practices of his fellow believers, he explains what happens when Christians meet together on Sundays:

And on the day called Sunday, all who live in cities or in the
country gather together to one place, and the memoirs of
the apostles or the writings of the prophets are read . . . then the
president verbally instructs, and exhorts to the imitation of these
good things. Then we all rise together and pray, and . . . when
our prayer is ended, bread and wine and water are brought, and
the president in like manner offers prayers and thanksgivings . . .
and the people assent, saying Amen; and there is a distribution
to each, and a participation of that over which thanks have been
given, and to those who are absent a portion is sent by the
deacons. And they who are well to do, and willing, give what
each thinks fit; and what is collected is deposited with the
president, who succours the orphans and widows and those
who, through sickness or any other cause, are in want . . .
all who are in need. But Sunday is the day on which we all hold
our common assembly, because it is the first day on which God
. . . made the world; and Jesus Christ our Saviour on the same
day rose from the dead.[1]

The same pattern is being played out as in Acts – gathering
together, praying, breaking bread, and then expressing their
faith practically in sharing their goods and providing for the less
well off. For these early Christians there was no disconnect
between worship and life, no dichotomy between offering
prayer to God and exercising practical care for their neighbours,
no division between doing church and being a disciple. The two
things – the gathered church coming together for worship and
the dispersed disciples going out to change the world – were
inextricably linked together. The former provided the incentive
and the energy for the latter. Working out what it meant to be
a disciple was a direct result of worshipping together. To
imagine that we can have one without the other in our generation is to risk ending up with a private version of Christianity,

one which disregards the lessons of history and deprives itself of the sustenance of community.

Our church isn't really very big, probably about sixty of us on a good Sunday. To be honest, we're a motley crew. There are one or two who are successful in life; you could call them 'high achievers', I guess. But most of us are very 'ordinary' people. The building isn't anything special either. It's certainly not an architectural gem of any kind. None of that matters much, because it's my Christian family and it's very special to me. Like all families, of course, we have our moments. Sometimes it drives me nuts, to be honest. But we're growing up together and I love these people. They help me to put into practice what the pastor preaches. And they help me to see that I'm a long way from being the finished article as a disciple.
(Sam)

The new humanity

And that's only half the truth! Of course, we need to be part of the church in order to receive the instruction and to gain the strength to live effectively, but the task of the church is far bigger than just equipping individuals to live good lives. Rowan Williams, Archbishop of Canterbury, describes the church as 'God's Pilot Project for the human race'. In other words, the purpose of the church is to demonstrate to the world around just how God means human beings to live and work together.

God created us for community and intimacy – to be in meaningful and loving relationships with himself and with each other. Human sinfulness and selfishness have so damaged those relationships that our humanity is diminished and distorted. But through the life, death and resurrection of Jesus the divisions have been bridged and the barriers have been broken down. So again and again the New Testament speaks not just about individuals being forgiven and restored, but about the creation of a new community and a new humanity. Barriers of race, social status and gender have no relevance in the church (Galatians 3:28). Eugene Peterson's translation of Ephesians 2 in *The Message* gets right to the point. He captures something of the wonder of the change that has taken place to bring the church into being. Christianity is not so much a new religion, more a new race of people united through Jesus:

> The Messiah has made things up between us so that we're now together on this, both non-Jewish outsiders and Jewish insiders. He tore down the wall we used to keep each other at a distance. He repealed the law code that had become so clogged with fine print and footnotes that it hindered more than it helped. Then he started over. Instead of continuing with two groups of people separated by centuries of animosity and suspicion, *he created a new kind of human being, a fresh start for everybody.*
>
> Christ brought us together through his death on the Cross . . . Through him we both share the same Spirit and have equal access to the Father.   (Ephesians 2:14–18, *The Message*)

The mission of the church is to demonstrate by her corporate life to a watching and often disillusioned world what God intends for all people and what it means to be truly and fully human. Admittedly the church fulfils that calling only imperfectly. All too often relationships between individual Christians and between different church streams are contaminated by the failings and limitations of our old unregenerate humanity. Frequently we're tied to obsolete structures and archaic customs that obscure the image of the new humanity from the wider society in which we live. *But the answer is not to reject the church.*

Our task is to recommit to the church, to re-imagine it, and to re-create its institutions and traditions in forms and expressions that will communicate with and challenge the world around us.

I'm not a theologian so I can't easily put into words what's really happening at communion. It's a bit of a mystery to me, but I know that there's something real. It makes me feel stronger in my faith, closer to Jesus and closer to the folk around me at church. We had a discussion about it in our cell group the other night. Liz used the word 'ordinance' and said we do it mainly because Jesus said we should. Bert agreed and explained that it was a symbol to remind us of the death of Jesus. Lynne has a high church background and said it was more than just that, that somehow or other something happens in communion that doesn't happen at any other time. I'm not sure who's right or whether they're all right in a way. I do think that if Jesus told us to do it, and if the church has done it down through the ages, it must have some kind of deep purpose and power. Whatever it is and however it happens, it works and that's enough for me.
(Danny)

The central ceremony

That's not to say that we have to reinvent the church in every generation. We're part of an ancient family, linked to those first disciples, and to every generation of Christians since, by a common commitment to Jesus as Saviour and Lord. And we're never more conscious of belonging together than when we share food. Like all good families, of course, we do all kinds of other things that express our life together. But nothing strengthens our unity as much as when we gather round the table. Whenever Christians have met together for worship, 'the breaking of bread' has usually been at the centre. In fact, from the description in Acts, it seems that this was the case both when they met in some public setting and when they met in their homes. Every time they came together they would celebrate and commemorate that unforgettable moment when Jesus had shared the Passover meal with his disciples. As he passed the cup and broke the bread, the ancient celebration of God's deliverance of Israel from slavery in Egypt merged into a dramatic revelation of the purpose of his imminent death on the cross.

The first Christians were, of course, Jewish and they carried with them the traditions of their Jewish faith and the practices of the synagogue. One thing made their worship distinctly Christian, however. It was the fact that again and again they would do as Jesus had told his disciples to do, and would use a simple meal – the breaking of bread and the sharing of a cup of wine – to fix their attention on the life, death and resurrection of Jesus. Every time they did so they would, in effect, tell the gospel story and claim its blessings and benefits all over again. We variously call our re-enactment of that meal the Lord's Supper, Communion, the Breaking of Bread, or the Eucharist. However we describe it, it works on so many different levels to remind us that our worship is all about Jesus and what he has done for us.

Remembering our roots

The communion meal helps to fix in our minds that our faith is *not* rooted in some mystical experience or in some philosophical discovery that we've made. As we share the elements of bread and wine, we're reminded that Jesus himself took these things and gave them to his disciples as representations of his body and blood. More importantly, they focus our attention on the fact that Jesus himself really did share our humanity, that he really did die for us, and that he really did rise again from the dead. *Our salvation is anchored in something that really happened.* If someone asks me, in good evangelical parlance, 'When were you saved?' I can give them two answers. I can tell them about the time when, as a youngster, I stepped forward in response to an appeal and asked Jesus to be my Saviour and Lord. But I can also honestly say, 'I was saved two thousand years ago on a green hill just outside the city of Jerusalem.' Both answers are correct. My first answer, my *experience* of salvation, is true only because of the prior *event*, the death of Jesus at Calvary, that made it possible.

Receiving grace

Eating and drinking are basic human activities. Healthy physical life is possible only because of the nourishment we receive. We can't keep ourselves alive by willpower or effort. Indeed, life itself is something we neither earned nor won for ourselves. It's a wonderful and mysterious gift bestowed on us. In the same way, as we eat and drink at the Lord's Table, we acknowledge that God's grace – his undeserved kindness – is the foundation on which our faith is built. The forgiveness we've received, the new life in Christ we enjoy and the privilege of being disciples of Jesus – they're all the result of grace. Bill Hybels often tells people that the difference between the Christian gospel and mere religion is in the way you spell them! Then, when their puzzled expressions indicate that they're not quite sure what he means, he adds, 'Religion is spelled D-O, but the gospel is spelled D-O-N-E.' Communion spells out the same truth, not in words, but in the symbolism of bread and wine.

Recognizing the risen Jesus

One of the most vivid stories in the Gospels is that of the two disciples walking to Emmaus. Devastated by the death of Jesus, Cleopas and his companion are trudging the seven weary miles homeward when they're joined by an unrecognized traveller.

As they talk together, his understanding of Scripture and his insightful words begin to bring some comfort. So, when they reach home, they offer him their hospitality for the night. The climax of the story comes when they sit down together to supper. Their guest becomes the host and the unknown traveller is recognized for who he really is:

> When he was at the table with them, he took bread, gave thanks, broke it and began to give it to them. Then their eyes were opened and they recognised him, and he disappeared from their sight. They asked each other, 'Were not our hearts burning within us while he talked with us on the road and opened the Scriptures to us?'
>
> They got up and returned at once to Jerusalem . . .
> (Luke 24:30–33)

The fact that Jesus disappeared from their sight would have added rather than detracted from the wonder of the event. They knew that this was no ghost: disembodied spectres don't sit at the table and break bread! But they were also discovering that he had conquered death and broken through to a new reality of life where his body was not subject to the limitations of our present time and space. The two weary disciples hot-footed it back to Jerusalem to share their discovery, energized by their realization that *even when his physical presence wasn't evident to them*, Jesus was still with them. One of the reasons Luke tells us that story is to remind us that it's at communion, when we share the bread and wine and remember Jesus' sacrifice, that we recognize more clearly what is true at every moment: *the crucified but risen Lord is with us!*

Relating to each other

Have you ever eaten in a really nice restaurant on your own? However good the food is, it's a very unsatisfactory experience.

Eating isn't just about satisfying your hunger. It needs company and conversation to be truly fulfilling. Exactly the same thing is true about communion. It's a shared experience, an expression of unity and fellowship. It involves and enhances our relationships with our fellow disciples who share the same grace and follow the same calling as we do. That's why Paul has such strong words for the church at Corinth. They had turned the communion meal into an orgy of eating and drinking. Instead of being a coming together, it was a cause of division:

> I hear that when you come together as a church, there are
> divisions among you . . . When you come together, it is not the
> Lord's Supper you eat, for as you eat, each of you goes ahead
> without waiting for anybody else. One remains hungry, another
> gets drunk. Don't you have homes to eat and drink in? Or do
> you despise the church of God and humiliate those who have
> nothing? What shall I say to you? Shall I praise you for this?
> Certainly not!   (1 Corinthians 11:18–22)

C. S. Lewis once used the phrase 'solemn fun' when talking about the Christian life. It's a particularly apt phrase to describe communion. To recall and re-enact the sacrificial death of Jesus is a solemn matter and we should always do so with a proper dignity and sense of awe. But it should also have all the joy of a family celebration as we affirm our commitment to Jesus and to the family of believers. As in all the best family gatherings, tears and laughter should never be far apart at communion.

Returning creation to God

Often communion is referred to as the 'eucharist', a word derived from the Greek word *eucharisteo*, meaning 'to give thanks'. It's the word that's used by both Mark and Paul when they describe the action of Jesus at his final meal on the night before he died. Before he broke the bread and passed the cup he 'gave thanks' (Mark 14:23–24; 1 Corinthians 11:23–24). This was the traditional Jewish practice at all meals and was a grateful acknowledgment that all things come from God, who created a good world for us to enjoy. To make such an acknowledgment involves a recognition that we are stewards of creation and that the ultimate purpose of any act of worship is to offer not only ourselves, but this creation back to God for his purposes.

Christians in the Orthodox tradition have grasped this more fully than we in the Western Church have done. Alexander Schmemann, a leading Orthodox theologian, saw in the powerful symbolism of the communion service that same call for all human beings to be like priests, offering ourselves and our world back to the One who created us. As we do so, our lives are an echo of Christ whose sacrifice on the cross offered not just his own life, but the whole of creation back to his Father:

> Only bread and wine: very ordinary things . . . according to the mind of the Church our initial offering in the Eucharist is not merely two things (bread and wine) but also our whole world, our whole life in all its dimensions . . . The world was God's gift to us, existing not for its own sake but in order to be transformed, to become life, and so to be offered back as man's gift to God . . . If, therefore, we remember our nature and our origins, we shall see in that bread and wine placed upon the altar not merely our individual selves but the whole world . . . We place ourselves and the world upon the altar . . . and see the Christ: He stands at the center and offers all to the Father.[2]

Reaching for the future

Communion connects us to the events of the past on which our faith is founded – to the death and resurrection of Jesus. It also confronts us with the challenge of the present – an encounter with the risen Jesus and a commitment to our fellow believers. It also comforts us with a promise – the promise that he will come again. That's why, having written so sternly about their abuses, Paul includes these tantalizing words in his instructions to the church in Corinth regarding communion: 'For whenever you eat this bread and drink this cup, *you proclaim the Lord's death until he comes*' (1 Corinthians 11:26, italics mine). Our experience when we come together in commemoration of Jesus' death and in celebration of his risen presence is but a shadow of what we will one day enjoy at his promised return. Then we'll be the guests at his great messianic banquet when all wrongs have been put right and his kingdom has come in all its fullness. The bread and wine are just a foretaste of all that's to come, a stimulus to hope that a broken world will one day be made perfect and whole.

The bonds of family

Some years ago my wife and I were asked to relocate to the USA to lead a congregation in Southern California. It meant leaving our daughters – both of whom were at college – in England. But, having discussed it as a family, we all felt it right for us to accept the assignment. After we'd been there a few months, Catriona and Jeni came out to spend a holiday with us. The time passed all too quickly and we had very mixed feelings as we shared a meal together on their last evening, knowing that in twenty-four hours we'd be a very long way apart again. But as we sat at the table, Margaret did something that neither they nor I will ever forget. She gave them each a front-door key for our house in California, telling them that although they might be more than 5,000 miles away, this was their home, that we'd always be expecting them, and that they should always feel welcome. It was a simple action and yet it said so much. It reminded us of what binds us together as a family and of how much we matter to each other. And it meant that every time we did something as basic as opening or closing the front door, we looked forward to being together again. Those keys became for all of us a sign of our unity as a family and a symbol of hope for the future.

Sometimes when I lay half asleep in the warm stillness of a Californian night, I would think of our girls back in the UK and of the keys that Margaret had given them. It might just have been the wind rustling in the trees outside our bedroom window, but I would fancy that I could hear a key slipped gently into the lock, the front door easing slowly open, footsteps echoing in the hallway. It was a dream, of course, *but it wasn't just wishful thinking*. It was the anticipation of reunion that kept us going and kept us close to each other through the long months of separation. And one day, when we least expected it, they surprised us by turning up just as we'd hoped and just as they'd promised! The Lord whom we serve and who has shown us the key of the communion meal will do no less than that.

Going Deeper

1. Frustration with the church as a 'gathered community' is not new. The writer of the letter to the Hebrews in the New Testament has to remind his readers of their responsibilities in this regard: 'Let us not give up meeting together, as some are in the habit of doing, but let us encourage one another . . . ' (Hebrews 10:25). John Wesley challenged the early Methodists with the words, 'God knows nothing of solitary religion.'

   What are the reasons in our generation that lead people to minimize the need to meet with other Christians in worship?

2. Many Baptist churches subscribe to a covenant which includes these words:

We engage therefore, by the aid of the Holy Spirit to walk together in Christian love; to strive for the advancement of this church, in knowledge, holiness, and comfort; to promote its prosperity and spirituality; to sustain its worship, ordinances, discipline, and doctrines; to contribute cheerfully and regularly to the support of the ministry, the expenses of the church, the relief of the poor, and the spread of the gospel through all nations.

How important is it to belong to a local fellowship of Christians? Can you come up with ten reasons for being part of a church?

6. A dying community

Today is dying day

On 22 October 1965 the renowned German scholar Paul Tillich realized that he had not long to live. Despite his international reputation as one of the leading theologians of the twentieth century, he hadn't always been a faithful husband. But in those last hours he asked his wife not to leave his side, and as she sat with him he sought and received her forgiveness for his unfaithfulness. Then she brought him his Greek New Testament and his German Bible, the things he prized most of all his possessions, just so that he could touch them. Together husband and wife repeated a short poem that they had often recited to each other. These were very precious and intensely private moments, and we can only imagine the conversation between a couple who were experiencing the healing of their relationship in the midst of the pain of parting. Perhaps the most poignant words spoken by Tillich that day were in the briefest of sentences when he said simply, 'Today is dying day.'[1]

We live at a time when thousands in the West are turning their backs on organized Christianity. Despite their fascination with Jesus, they believe the church has been as unfaithful to the gospel as any straying husband. Their suspicions will not be allayed by a clever public relations strategy or another outreach initiative. The words of Paul Tillich are applicable to the church in our day. *Today is dying day.* If we settle for merely circling the wagons and trying to protect what we've got, it could be the slow, lingering death of near extinction. But that isn't the only kind of death. The truth that we recognized in chapter 2 – that following Jesus involves a willingness to die – is as valid for the church as a whole as it is for individual disciples. *The call of the gospel is for us to be willing to die in order to live.*

Being an authentic disciple of Jesus demands a commitment to the community of believers. That means we have to be concerned for the health of the church. It certainly doesn't imply that we have to be satisfied with the status quo. Together we need to build a church that's willing to give up everything for the sake of the gospel. This isn't a time for tweaking procedures. This isn't a moment for modifying the machinery of church life. This isn't a problem that can be solved by new programmes. *This is a day for dying!* A day in which the church places everything – its time-honoured traditions, its ecclesiastical systems, its decision-making processes, its governing structures, its past successes, its treasured denominational distinctives – on the altar of mission. It will be far from easy and some good things may even be lost in the process. But in the economy of the gospel, it's only the willingness to die that leads to the wonder of resurrection. Imagine what that might mean for the church in our day. Imagine the transformation that would result.

I'd been attending the church for about a month when the pastor invited me to have coffee with him. I really appreciated the invitation. After we'd got through the initial small talk, it became apparent why he wanted to meet. I can still recall his words: 'It's great to have you worshipping with us. I hope you're going to settle in the church. Now what can we get you to do? I hear you enjoy singing and we need a good tenor in the choir.' He was very friendly and I know he meant well, but I knew this wasn't the kind of church I needed. We didn't talk about discipleship. And he didn't ask me anything about how God was using me in my everyday life or what challenges I was facing. His entire focus was on the church and its programmes. What happened in the rest of the week – which, of course, is by far the greater part of my life – didn't interest him at all.
(Peter)

Dying to maintenance and rising to mission

I once had a conversation with an irate member of my congregation who wanted to tell me why he felt that our church shouldn't change. 'I want my kids to be able to take part in all the activities that I did while I was growing up,' he said. He even had a neat little slogan: 'In this church *we want to preserve an expression.*' It sounded tidy enough – but it was all about maintenance, keeping the system ticking over and the programmes running smoothly. Unfortunately, over the years the world had changed and so had a younger generation who'd grown up in that church and voted with their feet.

I've also spoken with people who are more enlightened and who've moved beyond a maintenance mentality to a more marketing mindset. Undoubtedly, we've benefited from the insights of seeker-friendly churches in North America. It's right to ask whether our worship is meaningful to the person attending for the first time. We want newcomers to feel welcome and at home. But seeker-friendly churches work best in a culture where church attendance is still a part of normal life for ordinary people, and where their family may have stopped attending in their own lifetime or that of their parents. It's a marketing-based strategy, built around the concept of making the product better in order to attract the potential audience who have at least some predisposition to buy in.

It doesn't go nearly far enough in secularized, postmodern Europe. There are millions of people who've had little involvement with church – apart from weddings, christenings and funerals – for several generations. Improving the product won't cut it with people who don't even know we've got a product that might be of any interest to them. The unrelenting decline of many mainline denominations – some of which have valiantly made a succession of attempts to tighten their administrative structures, to brighten up their image, and to take on board the latest idea for growth – is clear evidence that a marketing approach won't work.

What we need is a renewed sense of the mission of the church – and that means far more than simply working harder to reach people with the gospel. One of the most significant new directions in recent years has been a more considered emphasis on the nature of mission. We've begun to realize that, above everything else, God is the God of mission – his great overarching mission to renew his entire creation. The mission of Israel as his 'chosen people' was to display his nature and purposes to the nations around them. Jesus came into the world to fulfil that mission and to bring God's great salvation to every nation on earth. The church exists to share in God's redemptive mission for his entire creation. To use Chris Wright's memorable phrase, 'It is not so much that God has a mission for his church in the world, as that God has a church for his mission in the world.'[2] To participate in the mission of God will mean much more than improving our evangelistic techniques or making our worship more contemporary and relevant.

Dying to invitation and rising to incarnation

It means changing the question from the one that we've got used to asking: How do we get people to come to church? The fact is that most of them just aren't coming. If we read the New Testament, we shouldn't be surprised at that. The words of Jesus that we call 'the Great Commission' confront us with a different challenge and force us to answer a different question. It's not about how we persuade people to come and join us. The question is this: How do we *go to people* with the good news? 'Then Jesus came to them and said, "All authority in heaven and on earth has been given to me. Therefore *go* and make disciples of all nations"' (Matthew 28:18–19, italics mine).

That's not to say that there isn't a place for invitation. Many of Jesus' greatest sayings are couched in the form of just such an invitation for people to come to him. But what we've too easily missed is the fact that such an *invitation* came only after his *incarnation*. It was only because he'd come among us, become one of us, shared our humanity to the point of suffering and even death, that he could then graciously invite us to come to him.

The church that truly shares in God's mission needs to follow that model. It needs to be an incarnational church, learning how to be fully involved in the problems and needs of the people and the communities who are its neighbours. It can't be a community that nostalgically longs for the past ages of Christendom in which the church had status and power. It can't be a community that simply 'does good' to the less fortunate in a paternalistic manner from a platform of privilege and a safe place of security. It can't be a community that is content to declare absolute truths from a position of moral and spiritual superiority. The incarnational church will empty itself of social and cultural privileges in order to be a truly missional community. It will welcome all who want to be part of its fellowship. Rather than judging its success solely by the numbers attending its services, it will see its purpose fulfilled in those who are intentionally serving others in the name of Christ.

Most people would describe my fifteen years of ministry as successful. The congregation grew and we developed some very innovative pro-grammes in evangelism and social care. But when I took time off on sabbatical I had an uneasy feeling about it all. The more I reflected on it, the more clearly I came to see what was missing. I realized that I just wasn't creating a system that intentionally produced disciples. I had created a centralized missional station to do mission. The intention was mission and discipleship was just a by-product. It was like I was driving a big 'mission truck' with a follow-up 'discipleship van'. People were busy doing good stuff, but I don't think they were necessarily growing spiritually. And they weren't being equipped for living as followers of Jesus outside the church activities. When I go back I want it to be different. Now I want to create spiritual formation within the mission so that making disciples is at the heart of all we do.
(Edward)

Dying to membership and rising to discipleship

The church that's focused on mission will care more about making disciples than about making members. When formal membership is the primary consideration, the emphasis falls on recruiting and retaining people. What matters more than anything else is increasing the attendances and sustaining the activities that take place within the four walls of the church. I once visited a pastor who said that he could easily sum up the nature of his task. 'It boils down to just two things,' he told me confidently. 'I want to grow this church and populate heaven!' But that's a terribly reductionist version of the gospel – filling the pews and preparing people for paradise. It's all but lost sight of the fact that the mission of the church is not just to rescue individuals from hell, but to enlist them in God's great project of redemption.

There are two things we need to get clear in our thinking. First, if Jesus is Lord of every area of life and if God's mission is to renew his entire creation, then the division of life into the *sacred* (the 'religious' part) and the *secular* (what we do with the rest of our lives) is false. Second, we need to take seriously the time we spend in activities that aren't church based – in other words, the time we spend at home, at work and in leisure pursuits. Think about how you spend a typical week. You'll need to spend around 48 hours getting some much-needed sleep. That leaves you with 120 hours. Even if you're a very committed church member (unless you're retired with lots of discretionary time), the maximum time you'll spend in church-based activities will be about 10 hours in a week. That leaves 110 hours which you'll spend with your family, earning a living, following some leisure pursuits or just getting on with the normal chores of life. *And that's where we need to learn to live as authentic followers of Jesus.*

'Whole-life discipleship' is how it's sometimes described and churches need to become whole-life-disciple-making communities, equipping people for the 110 hours when they're not in church. Far from reducing the significance of the 'gathered church', it actually increases its importance. What we do when we come together as church becomes even more vital when we realize the importance of discipling every individual in the gathered community. They will have an impact far beyond the walls of the church and its immediate environs. Those 50, or 100, or 200 people who meet on a Sunday will be scattered far and wide throughout the rest of the week. They'll certainly find themselves in very different and sometimes very difficult situations – and the number of people whose lives they will touch may well number into the thousands.

If we view them as just church members, it's enough to *recruit and retain* them. All we need to do is to find out what their gifts and talents are and put them to work in church activities. But if we understand that every one of them is a 'whole-life disciple' of Jesus, then our task is to *resource and release* them. The questions become much more searching and the task becomes much more far-reaching. Leaders begin to ask:

- 'What's God doing in your life?'
- 'How is God using you at work?'
- 'What are the challenges you're facing at home?'
- 'How can we support you on your front line of discipleship?'
- 'How can we pray for you at this time?'
- 'Can I spend some time at your place of employment so that I understand what you do?'
- 'What are the areas of life in which you feel in need of deeper and more relevant Christian teaching?'
- 'What issues do the movies you're watching and the books you're reading raise in relation to your faith?'
- 'Are we asking too much of you in terms of responsibilities in the church?'

When we ask and respond to those questions, churches begin to change. Worship has a deeper dimension as people bring every aspect of their lives and make them an offering to God. The preaching of the Word has a wider relevance as it's applied to every situation and relationship. The understanding of the work of the church expands to include not only the fellowship that the believers share with each other and the ministry that the church exercises in the immediate community through its outreach and caring programmes, but also the work and witness of each person in his or her daily life and occupation.

A couple of years ago I didn't know that churches like ours existed. The only church I knew was the big building with the steeple at the end of our road. Most of the week it seemed to be closed. On Sunday mornings I'd see a handful of elderly people going in when I was out getting my Sunday papers. I got to know Ian at work and I'd always liked him. He seemed the kind of guy you could trust. He and Beth had us round for supper one evening. It was only then that I discovered they were Christians. After that we had some interesting conversations about faith. What was intriguing about Ian was that he didn't argue about God. He didn't really seem all that religious, but he did talk naturally about being a follower of Jesus. I got more and more interested and he invited Kath and me to be part of a group that meets at their house a couple of times a month. The conversation was relaxed and nobody pressurized us. We've started going to their Sunday morning service. It's in a school hall near us, not in a church. I haven't sorted out exactly where I stand with it all, but I really like being part of it. It kind of sucks you in. I'm not sure where it'll all end up . . .
(Ron)

Dying to closed shop and rising to open house

The change of emphasis from recruiting and retaining members to resourcing and releasing disciples changes the very nature of the church community. When membership is the paramount thing, the community becomes a 'bounded set'. In other words, there's a clear distinction between those who are 'inside' and those who are on the 'outside' of the community. In order to belong you must give an undertaking that you subscribe to a statement of belief and to a standard of behaviour that together govern the life and define the character of the group. These may vary between different churches, but they always reflect what that particular church or denomination believes to be the teaching of the Bible.

When these are seen as guidelines they're extremely useful in making clear the values and beliefs of the Christian community. The problem arises when they become boundaries. The difficulty for newcomers is that it isn't possible for them to be part of the group until they've reached a point where they can assent to the conditions of membership. The challenge for long-time members is less immediately obvious, but just as real. Once you're 'in' the group, and as long as you can keep within the rules, you can settle very comfortably without deepening in your relationship with Jesus. Although leaders and members are often aware of these issues, they have an understandable fear that any other way of doing church would lead to a kind of spiritual anarchy in which everyone is free to believe what they like and do as they please. But when churches make discipleship their priority, there's a much healthier way open to the community.

Discipleship, as we've recognized, arises out of a gracious invitation from Jesus. When Peter, Andrew and the others began to follow Jesus they had little if any understanding of his identity as Lord and Messiah. Their behaviour was often as inappropriate as their beliefs were ill-formed. That remained the case long after they had responded to his initial call. One moment Peter, under the inspiration of the Spirit, was recognizing Jesus as the Christ; the next he was speaking words that Jesus knew came from the leadings of Satan (Matthew 16:13–23). Even as the shadow of the cross loomed over them and as they approached the final chapter of Jesus' life on earth, James and John were still failing to grasp all that Jesus had taught them as they sought the best places in his kingdom (Mark 10:35–45). But, however imperfectly, they kept following and that was what mattered most.

That little band of disciples who walked the dusty roads of first-century Palestine in the company of their rabbi is a perfect example of a 'centred set'. Their tiny community was not defined by boundaries of strict rules and perfectly articulated doctrine, but by the person and teaching of Jesus, on whom their lives were centred and focused. They weren't held together by rules and statements of belief, but by a loyalty to and a fascination with the person of Jesus. It didn't mean that they could believe what they liked or do as they pleased. What mattered, however, was not their duty to keep the rules, but their devotion to a relationship with Jesus. They provide us with a model for church that we have too long neglected.

To the majority of people in our culture, church is a 'closed shop', a place for the initiated and the religiously inclined. But in a postmodern, post-Christendom age in which the gospel story has been largely forgotten and long-cherished Christian standards are no longer the norm, there are many who are still fascinated by and drawn to the little they know of Jesus. If we're serious about discipleship we need to be committed to the task of building church communities where the boundaries have been removed, or at least lowered, and where everything is centred on the call of Jesus for us to follow him. Instead of 'closed shops' we need to create 'open houses' where anyone who's interested can have a sense of belonging while they begin to discover who Jesus is and what he is saying to them. What will hold everything together will not be the fixed boundaries of membership, but the shared focus on discipleship.

We began this chapter with a glimpse of the last hours – the dying day – of a brilliant but flawed individual. They were much more than the final moments of his life. They were moments of deep healing. They were also moments of preparation for a future that's unknown and even frightening. But it's a future that's also welcoming and liberating for everyone who walks towards it in the company of Jesus, who has already travelled that road. The prospect for the church is equally unknown. It's more than a little scary, for we know that our future will be very different from our present. But a church that's willing to die will find the healing it needs to be vigorous and effective. A church that's willing to die will also enjoy the welcoming presence of the risen Lord in a future that will hold new opportunities to worship and witness as the body of Christ.

Going Deeper

1. Put aside an evening to get together with a group of friends and dream of the kind of church God needs as we move through the first quarter of the twenty-first century. Don't be limited by 'what's possible', but dream big dreams and express your most extravagant longings for the church. Let the evening be a mixture of stillness, contemplation, prayer, conversation and healthy, holy hilarity. Before it ends, make sure that you write down all the dreams and hopes you've shared together.

2. Meet again a week or two later to look at the things you recorded in that meeting. Ask each other, 'What can we do *now* to move towards being a church like that?' Get it down

to six things you can do. Make sure that those six things are about 'what we can do together' and don't simply involve complaining about the church and blaming other people!

3. Get on with putting them into practice!

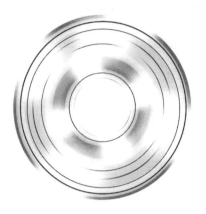

7. A learning community

Listening to the Master

Late one afternoon in the spring of 1928, two jazz instrument-alists were strolling through South Side Chicago. One was Bud Freeman, a young tenor saxophone player. Freeman, for all his exceptional talent, was in awe of his friend who, though still only twenty-six, had already become something of a legend to his admirers and a hero to his fellow musicians. As they turned a corner they chanced upon a group of buskers who were strug-gling manfully, if somewhat discordantly, through a popular jazz hit of the day – a tune with the splendid title of 'Struttin'

With Some Barbecue'. The two professional musicians stood and listened. When the last note sounded they joined in the applause of the small crowd that had gathered round.

That's when Freeman's companion walked towards the trumpet player. Not wishing to embarrass the well-meaning amateur, he whispered to him, 'Man, you're playing that too slow.'

The street musician wasn't overly impressed by this unsolicited critique of his playing from a total stranger. 'How would *you* know?' he immediately countered with more than a hint of annoyance in his voice.

'Well,' came the reply, 'I'm Louis Armstrong. That's my chorus you're playing.'

Suitably chastened and very impressed, the trumpet player readily accepted the counsel of his new-found mentor and the two men shook hands warmly.

The next day, at around the same time, Bud Freeman and Louis Armstrong found themselves again in the same street. And there was the same group of enthusiastic novices playing the same tune as they'd attempted just twenty-four hours earlier. This time there were two significant differences. The first was that they were playing the music just a little better than they had the day before. The second – and more noteworthy – change was that in front of their tin collecting cup they had propped a hastily handwritten notice. It read simply, 'PUPILS OF LOUIS ARMSTRONG'. They were still a long way short of perfection, but they wanted everyone to know that they were listening to and learning from the master. At the very least their audience would know what they were aiming for.

Churches are often at considerable pains to announce to the world their denominational allegiance and their doctrinal position, but how would it be if we took a leaf out of the book of those Chicago buskers from the 1920s? What if we got rid of those impressive titles above our doors and on our church noticeboards? What if we simply announced ourselves as *disciples*, or, to put it in the more familiar language of our day, *pupils* – or better still *apprentices – of Jesus Christ*? That's a description that would combine a holy audacity with a proper humility: the audacity to say that we're aiming at nothing less than living like Jesus, and the humility to acknowledge that we're still a long way short of being perfectly like our Master. How would that impact the kind of churches and Christian communities of which we're a part, if we really took that description seriously? Discipling would become the defining mark of church culture, the DNA that makes us who we are. It would become *the main thing*. And the only way to keep the main thing as the main thing would be for the church to be a learning community.

Learning together

Sometimes you hear people describe a church as having 'a good teaching ministry'. Usually they mean that the preaching is of a high standard or that they run some effective Bible study programmes. Admirable as those things are, we're missing something very important. It puts all the emphasis on the material being offered by the pastor rather than on the active participation of the entire congregation. I've yet to hear anyone speak admiringly of a church with 'a good learning ministry'. Contrast that with some key words in the description of the first group of believers in Acts: '*They devoted themselves to* the apostles' teaching and to the fellowship, to the breaking of bread and to prayer' (Acts 2:42, italics mine). The literal translation of the Greek is, 'they were *continuing steadfastly in* the teaching of the apostles'. Those early believers weren't just passive hearers of the pious exhortations of Peter and his fellow leaders. Nor were they even just the willing recipients of their instructions in Christian living. They were enthusiastically and persistently living *in* that teaching. This was a continuous process in which they were active learners rather than merely acquiescent listeners.

The learning cycle

We tend to think of learning as a purely intellectual exercise in which we memorize and master the contents of a book or the subject matter of a course of study. Real learning is more than that. It isn't just about 'knowing stuff'. We learn in order to live better, to be better people, to do better work. In recent years educationalists have analysed the learning process. In doing so they've visualized it as a cycle that begins with an *experience* – something that happens to us or something that we deliberately seek out. It may be a positive or a negative experience, but the point is that it provides a platform for learning and developing. In fact, everything that happens to us in life can become just such a learning experience. However, if real learning is to take place as a consequence of that experience, then it needs to be followed by a period of *reflection* – a time to look back at what actually happened. This will involve thinking carefully through all that took place and perhaps making notes. Certain *conclusions* can then be drawn in which we seek to discover the lessons to be learned for the future. The final stage involves drawing up a *plan* based on the conclusions reached so that we can handle similar situations better in the future. That, in turn, will lead to yet another experience as we seek to *apply* what's been learned. And so the learning process starts all over again.

This is how discipleship works. The stories of Jesus and his disciples in the Gospels provide us with abundant examples of this kind of active learning in operation. We see them in a whole variety of situations. Each one – whether it's being caught in a storm on a lake, trying unsuccessfully to cast out an evil spirit, or engaging in an unworthy dispute about who's the greatest – is an experience from which lessons can be drawn. Again and again we hear the words and witness the actions of Jesus as he stills the storm, rebukes their lack of faith, or explains the nature of true greatness. Just being with him, observing his actions and absorbing his teaching meant that they were constantly reflecting on and drawing conclusions from the tumultuous events that marked the three brief years they spent in his company. What they learned became the template for how they would live after his death and resurrection. The result was that a handful of very ordinary and very flawed men and women became the kind of disciples who changed the world by the message they shared and the lives they lived.

The challenge for us is to replicate their discipleship development in our day – to become intentional about disciple-making. It won't be enough for each of us individually to get serious about growing like Jesus and living for Jesus. You can't develop fully as a follower of Jesus on your own. It can't be done as an individual project devoted to the pursuit of personal piety. It involves meaningful relationships and mutual responsibilities with fellow believers. It takes a community of intentional believers to produce a disciple. You can't make fully formed disciples without a church and you can't have a properly functioning church without disciples. In such a disciple-making community a number of characteristics will be clearly present.

I grew up in the fiercely Protestant culture of Northern Ireland where there was an inbuilt suspicion of any kind of ritual or anything symbolic. I remember the outcry when our pastor had the idea of lighting Advent candles. One of the elders protested that it was the first step on the march to Rome – a denial of everything the Reformation had stood for. I think some of the congregation would have burned the pastor at the stake if they could have!

How things have changed! We do all sorts of things in our church these days. They really engage my imagination and sometimes they move me to tears. On Good Friday we took time to sit quietly and write down anything that caused us to feel guilty or resentful. Then one after another people went forward to the front of the church and nailed the pieces of paper to the cross. The sound of the hammering was eerie but wonderfully liberating. I think I understood the power of the cross for the very first time.
(Emily)

Meaning-filled rituals

Genuine learning engages the imagination as well as the intellect, being experienced by our senses as much as apprehended by our minds. That's why ritual and liturgy have an important place in the life of the church. The rhythmic language of a well-composed liturgy or the repeated action of a frequently used ritual do more than simply lodge themselves in the memory. They also enter our consciousness at a level that is deeper than mere rational thought or cold logic. They become part of who we are and give us mental and emotional 'hooks' on which to hang our thinking. Because we do them together, they also help to define our corporate identity. They're dramatic reminders that we're not on our own and that we belong to a community which is a source of strength and possesses a spring of deep and rich meaning.

Church is vital to the individual disciple, because it anchors each of us in a shared experience of truth that protects us from going off spiritually and theologically in all kinds of wrong directions. The principal rituals of baptism and communion are obvious examples of that, rooting us in the great certainties of the faith. But there are countless other rituals that serve to hold us together in fellowship and strengthen us for witness and service. Some, like reciting the creeds or making the sign of the cross, go back centuries. Others can be crafted as we affirm our faith in relevant symbols that help us face the challenges of our day. When I came to the end of a particular period of ministry, some friends organized a service in which the congregation were asked to pray for Margaret and me. It would have been impossible for two hundred people to pray publicly and many would have found it an ordeal to pray aloud. So everyone was asked to write their prayer or a verse of Scripture on a stone which they then placed in a glass jar. That jar now sits in our lounge and every time I handle those stones and read those prayers I'm deeply grateful for that simple but sensitive ritual.

Chris and I make a point of meeting once every two weeks, for coffee on a Saturday morning. At first it was fairly ad hoc and we'd just chat generally about trying to live as a Christian in our everyday lives. But, as we've gone on, it's got a bit more structured without being too rigid. We've homed in on four questions that we ask each other each time.

- *As a disciple of Jesus, what are the challenges you're facing at this time?*
- *As a disciple of Jesus, what are the opportunities opening up to you at this time?*
- *What steps are you taking to grow in holiness and Christ-likeness at this time?*
- *How is God speaking to you at this time?*

We don't give each other lots of advice. It's more that we encourage each other to be intentional in our discipleship and to take responsibility for what God wants us to do. Of course, we spend time praying together, but we also seem to spend a fair bit of time laughing together.

It's a serious business, but not at all solemn or artificially pious. I think we both feel it helps us enormously.
(Raymond)

Mentoring relationships

When churches take disciple-making seriously, the old paradigm, in which the entire responsibility for spiritual formation was placed on the shoulders of just one leader, will no longer be adequate. Of course, depending on the size of the church and the way in which it's structured, an individual may well be charged with overseeing and providing resources for this aspect of ministry, but the responsibility must be shared by every believer. There's no place for the individualistic concept of 'every man for himself' when it comes to discipleship. Being a disciple involves both being nurtured and nurturing others.

The word 'mentor' came into the English language from Greek mythology to describe someone who provides guidance and practical support to another person, particularly in times of crisis or through stages of significant development. But it's a concept that's thoroughly biblical in its meaning. In the story of Israel's exodus from Egypt, Jethro acts as a mentor to his son-in-law Moses, providing him with good advice on how to lead and administer justice to his people (Exodus 18:13–26). The prophet Elijah mentors Elisha as he prepares him to be his successor (1 Kings 19:19–21). In the New Testament Paul fulfils a mentoring role towards the younger man Timothy, whom he considered as 'my true son in the faith' (1 Timothy 1:2). And, of course, the relationship of Jesus to the twelve men who shared his three years of public ministry was primarily that of a mentor, as he led them to spiritual maturity and prepared them to build his church after his resurrection and ascension.

It's no exaggeration to say that the practice of mentoring lies at the very heart of disciple-making.

Many churches recognize the importance of getting people into small groups which provide a depth of fellowship and an opportunity for Bible study that is impossible in a larger congregation. What isn't always so readily understood is that these closer relationships are vital to making disciples. Either one on one, or in groups of three or four, people need to have an accountability to each other and a responsibility for each other. These relationships will involve praying and reading the Bible together, but they also need to find time and space for encouraging each other in following Jesus in all the normal activities of life. To create that time and space may well mean reducing the number of church activities. It may mean reordering the priorities and even totally reshaping the way in which the church is structured. But without such mutually beneficial mentoring relationships it will be difficult to put disciple-making at the heart of the life of our churches.

Monologues and responses

We've already acknowledged that good preaching alone will not be sufficient to create a learning community that produces authentic disciples. Some would even go so far as to suggest that preaching – as traditionally understood – has no place in today's church. We can readily agree that there's no place for preaching that's ill-prepared, poorly delivered, biblically unsound or lacking in application to the needs and challenges that people face in their everyday lives. It's also difficult to argue against the premise that certain styles of rhetoric and communication are ill-suited to our times. Like it or not, we're in the age of the persuasive soundbite and the powerful visual image. We don't need to uncritically follow every trend and fashion in communication, but nor can we blithely ignore them in the matter of preaching. We need to be careful, however, that we don't make the mistake of discarding a vital and God-given means of preparing God's people for the task of mission in the world. The purpose of successful teaching of any kind is to create an environment in which everyone involved is able to learn effectively. Good preaching can function in precisely that manner – provided we remember a number of key things.

Preaching is intended to *instruct* the hearers in the truths of the Bible. A major part of the preacher's task is the careful study of the meaning of a passage of Scripture and deep reflection on its message and application for today. The man or woman assigned the duty of preaching is charged with the responsibility of spending time on behalf of the rest of us in order to bring us to a deeper understanding of the things we need to know to live better. But preaching can also *inspire* us. At its best, and under the inspiration of the Holy Spirit, it's uniquely effective at this. The combination of divine truth, communicated in carefully chosen words, through a personality that's marked by a passion for the gospel and an integrity in Christian living, results in a drama that's inspiring and motivating. It's no coincidence that the most gifted practitioners of the art of preaching have a love of stories and a facility to tell them in a way that can captivate the attention of listeners. At its heart, all effective preaching is story-telling. And the story that it tells is the one great love story of a God who would give up his own Son for a lost world. It's a tragedy and a travesty that we've managed to tell that story so often without moving every hearer to tears of repentance and whoops of joy.

In a learning community there's a third objective for preaching, an objective that it's often failed to fulfil. It must *initiate a conversation*: the monologue of the preacher must lead to a dialogue in which everyone has something to say. A church that wants to be a learning community needs to make time for reflection in the limited hours its congregation are gathered together. That time will be characterized by the kind of questions that lead to action:

- 'What does this mean for us today?'
- 'What do we need to do about this?'
- 'Is there anything that needs to change?'
- 'Do we need to hear more on this subject?'
- 'Can we discern clear themes emerging as we submit to the authority of God's Word?'

The suggestion that it might be good for churches to 'have one well-prepared sermon each month and spend four weeks reflecting together on its implications'[1] might well be worthy of consideration.

The ultimate purpose of the sermon, however, is not to provide food for thought or topics for lively debate. The call of the gospel is for us to be *doers* of the Word rather than merely hearers. *We're apprentices, not academics.* Preaching should *inform our living.* The challenge to the preacher is to deliver the good news in such a way that the hearers are equipped to live good lives for God in the world. The real question for any preacher on any Sunday in any church is this: How will this help these people and how can they translate it into action this time tomorrow morning? That, in truth, is the point of everything the church does as a learning community. The Word of God – written in Scripture, delivered by the preacher, discussed and digested by the body of believers, enacted in all our rituals – needs to be made flesh in the life of every disciple.

The bottom line

Eugene Peterson was once asked about how we learn to pray. Perhaps surprisingly, he didn't recommend a book or suggest a course in the spiritual disciplines. He just said, 'If someone comes to me and says, "Teach me how to pray," I say, "Be at this church at nine o'clock on Sunday morning." That's where you learn how to pray.'[2] The truth for all followers of Jesus is that it's only in the community of believers that we can fully experience the deepest realities of the gospel and learn to express them in our daily lives. The challenge for the church is to be a genuine fellowship of learners, a place where the youngest to the oldest would be happy to describe themselves as *pupils of Jesus Christ*.

Going Deeper

1. Take time to share with a group of trusted fellow disciples a recent *experience* that has been particularly significant for you. It may even be helpful to re-enact the incident with one of the group in the form of a role play.

   Then spend some time with the group in *reflection* on the experience. What really happened? Was there anything happening 'under the surface' that you might not have noticed at the time? What was positive and what was negative? What difference did the fact that you are a disciple of Jesus make in this situation?

   What *conclusions* can you draw from it? Is there anything in the Bible that would be particularly relevant to the situation and that would help you? Make a list of two or three big lessons that you can learn.

   Finally, draw up a simple *plan* as to how you might put those lessons into practice in the future.

2. Here's a simple technique that you might use in working through with a mentor how you, as a disciple, might deal with a difficult situation.

   a) *The challenge*. Take time to talk through the situation in question. The task of the mentor is not to give you lots of advice, but to help you articulate and face up to the issue. Sometimes the real problem lies beneath the surface and conversation helps bring that out.

b) *The chain.* In every situation there's a 'chain' – the *problem* itself; the other *people* involved, for example workmates, family members, other people at church; the person, namely *you*, facing that problem. It helps to think how these all interact together.

c) *The choices.* What can you do in each of these links in the chain? What can you do to deal directly with the *problem*? What do you need to do with regard to the other *people* involved? Is there a difficult conversation you need to have? Do you need to apologize or repair a relationship? And – most important of all – what about *you*? What is all this telling you about your progress as a disciple? Is there something that needs to change in you?

8. A witnessing community

Geoff makes a point of going to church wherever he happens to be. That's why he found himself as part of a small rural congregation one Sunday morning in the middle of winter. He arrived early and took his place in a pew. No-one spoke to him, although he did find a somewhat yellowed and dog-eared sheet of A4 paper that included the information that coffee was available after the service. By the end of the none-too-inspiring hour he was feeling cold and very much in need of the promised warm beverage. Since none of his fellow worshippers volunteered the information as to where refreshments were being served, he plucked up his courage and asked the person who was tidying up the hymn books. 'Well,' she replied, with a knowing look and in a voice just above a whisper, 'we usually wait until any visitors have gone.' Geoff took the hint, hurried back to his car, and sought the sanctuary of the local pub. The warm glow of a log fire and the welcoming buzz of conversation were infinitely preferable to the grudging fellowship of the church he'd just left.

Fortunately not all churches are like that. There are many – large and small, long established and newly planted, traditional and contemporary in their style of worship – that seek to reach out to their communities. Few would have the narrow vision and smug self-satisfaction that Geoff encountered on that cold winter's day. Yet it's all too easy to settle for something far less – far duller and more monochrome – than the glorious picture of the church painted for us in Scripture. The fact that so many who are drawn to Jesus are repelled by what they see of the church confronts us with a painful possibility: what they're rejecting may be a distorted and diminished caricature of the biblical model of the church. They may, by their rejection of the status quo, be challenging us to be more faithful to what the church is really called to be.

A church for all eternity

In his letter to the church in Ephesus, Paul writes about his calling to preach to both Jews and Gentiles. His commission is to declare God's great purpose to redeem fallen humanity and to restore his broken creation. Until the life, death and resurrection of Jesus, he explains, this was a 'mystery' – a plan hidden deep in the heart of God himself. But now it's being revealed to the entire created universe, and the means by which it's to be communicated is through the corporate life and witness of God's new community, the church:

Although I am less than the least of all God's people, this grace was given me: to preach to the Gentiles the unsearchable riches of Christ, and to make plain to everyone the administration of this mystery, which for ages past was kept hidden in God, who created all things. His intent was that now, through the church, the manifold wisdom of God should be made known to the rulers and authorities in the heavenly realms, according to his eternal purpose which he accomplished in Christ Jesus our Lord. (Ephesians 3:8–11)

Those striking words contain some truths about the extravagant nature of grace and the exhilarating role of the church that offer a blueprint for the church in every age.

The multiracial welcome of grace

Paul's letter was written from prison and in a few brief words he reminds his readers precisely why he's suffering such incarceration. He's a 'prisoner of Christ Jesus for the sake of you Gentiles' (Ephesians 3:1). God's grace, he's convinced, was shown to him precisely so that he might 'preach to the Gentiles the unsearchable riches of Christ'. The essence of the 'mystery' that God has revealed to him is the truth that the old barrier between the Jews, as God's chosen people, and non-Jews (the Gentiles) no longer exists. God's grace is for all nations and all peoples on earth. Those who put their faith in Jesus, whatever their ethnic origin, are united with him and with each other. The Gentiles, he insists, are 'heirs together with Israel, members together of one body, and sharers together in the promise in Christ Jesus' (Ephesians 3:6). Differences of race, colour and culture count for nothing in the church, the most inclusive and international community on earth.

That gloriously positive truth holds a twofold warning to every church and to every individual follower of Jesus. Churches which limit that unconditional welcome of grace to their 'own kind' deny their very purpose. The presence of the Black Majority churches in Britain is a lasting reminder that in the 1960s a generation of Afro-Caribbean immigrants encountered a predominantly white church that, with few exceptions, failed to embrace them as brothers and sisters in Christ. Those Black Majority churches greatly enrich the life of the church in Britain today by their vibrancy and their numerical strength. Nonetheless, their very existence is a condemnation of a church that lacked the divine grace and the common humanity to open its heart and its doors to the strangers who came to live next door. It's a sin that we must never repeat if the church is to have any credibility in a world which longs to see barriers of race and gender destroyed.

There's an equally serious warning to those who would too readily give up on the church. We deny the transforming and reconciling power of the gospel if we think we can 'go it alone', or if we're willing to find fellowship only with a handful of kindred spirits who see things our way. Race and colour are not the only things that divide Christians. We separate too easily over styles of worship, nuances of doctrine, differences of church governance, half-forgotten hurts of history and long-remembered personal slights. If we can't or won't worship and work together as disciples of Jesus, then we've nothing to offer a fractured and fallen world. The same grace that uncondition-ally accepts us uncompromisingly demands our allegiance to the body of Christ.

The multicoloured wisdom of God

The importance that Paul placed on the church is nowhere more clearly stated than in his assertion that it's 'through the church' that the 'manifold wisdom of God should be made known'. The Greek word rendered 'manifold' in English literally means 'many coloured', a wonderfully expressive word that was used to describe extravagantly coloured flowers or richly embroidered cloths. It's particularly evocative when it's employed as an adjective to illustrate the wisdom of God. For Paul, divine wisdom is something very different from merely human intelligence. The wisdom of God is to be seen not only in his just laws or in his magnificent creation. It is supremely displayed in his plan to redeem and renew that creation, and particularly in the life, death and resurrection of Jesus Christ. When he writes to the Corinthians, Paul describes Jesus as both 'the power of God and the wisdom of God . . . our righteousness, holiness and redemption' (1 Corinthians 1:24, 30). The 'many coloured wisdom' of God is *everything that we see in Jesus*, everything that's available to us through his sacrificial death and risen presence – a rich and glorious tapestry of love and grace.

How is that to be made known today? Paul has no doubt that it must be *through the church*. No one person, however gifted, can possibly contain within himself all that God has revealed in Jesus. No one group of Christians, however fervent or committed, can communicate to others such a masterpiece of divine revelation. It will be glimpsed by a watching world only as it's displayed on the vast canvas of the church with its vibrant and colourful array of cultures, races, personalities, giftings and ministries. The gospel of Jesus can never be the monopoly of one denomination, the grace of God can never be fully expressed in one doctrinal statement, the Great Commission can never be fulfilled by one evangelistic strategy, and the glory of the King of kings can never be confined to one place, one race or one time.

There's only one church, one great panorama of worshippers and witnesses stretched across the centuries. Every individual follower of Jesus and every group of believers is committed to be part of it, to share its mission and to demonstrate its beauty in their local situation. Just as the New Testament letters are addressed to the church in Rome, Corinth or Galatia, we're called to be the church where we are. In our corporate life our neighbours should catch a glimpse of the new world order in which God's kingdom holds sway and where his will is perfectly done. In the beauty of our worship, in the values we embrace, in the way we relate to each other, in the way we impact our little bit of the world, and in the grace that characterizes everything we do – in all this the church must be the evidence that God is love, that Jesus is alive, and that the Holy Spirit is moving to renew and heal a broken creation.

The multidimensional witness of the church

Paul has still further to go in his exploration of the magnitude of the role of the church in God's plan. Look again at the final sentence in the passage: 'His intent was that now, through the church, the manifold wisdom of God should be made known to the rulers and authorities in the heavenly realms, according to his eternal purpose which he accomplished in Christ Jesus our Lord' (Ephesians 3:10–11). His assertion is breathtaking in its audacity. The church is the living organism in and through which God has chosen to announce and demonstrate his salvation to the whole created order – *including the angelic creation!* As one commentator has memorably expressed it, 'the history of the Christian church becomes a graduate school for angels'.[1] Indeed, the church and its vital role, Paul tells us, have been in the mind and the will of God for all eternity.

It's worth remembering that Paul was the last man to see the church through rose-tinted spectacles. He knew the hard realities of church life as much as we do. He suffered at the hands of fellow believers whose view of the gospel was so circumscribed that they would have limited salvation only to those who first adopted the legal demands of Judaism. His letters bear witness to the fact that the churches he founded often lapsed into heretical beliefs and seriously immoral behaviour. In one deeply personal passage he catalogues some of the more painful experiences of his missionary life – imprisonment, beatings, shipwreck, constant travel, relentless criticism, exhaustion, hunger and deprivation – only to climax this litany of calamities with some heart-rending words on the costliest aspect of all in his ministry: 'Besides everything else, I face daily the pressure of my concern for all the churches' (2 Corinthians 11:28). But that didn't for one minute alter the fact that, for Paul, the church was God's chosen instrument to declare his salvation across time and eternity. Nor did it lessen his passionate love for the church. Despite our frustrations with the church in our day, we should do no less than follow Paul's example. When we do that, we discover that loving the church is far from being an exclusive commitment to those who are believers. It will mean a compassion for the world to whom the church is called to witness and for whom the church is charged to care.

More than a decade ago, I attended a conference at Willow Creek Church in Chicago. In one of the sessions Bill Hybels spoke of being involved in a conflict resolution meeting at a church for which he had a pastoral concern. When the meeting was over, he had gone to a nearby coffee shop feeling drained by his efforts to bring some level of reconciliation. As he sat there he took his journal and, despite the frustration of the meeting he had just left, he wrote five simple words, 'I just love the church.' It was one of those wonderful moments when I felt that I was the only person in the auditorium and that those words were being addressed just to me. Tears began to run down my cheeks and for two or three hours I cried in a way that I haven't done at any other time in my life. I can only describe the experience as a kind of baptism of love for the church.

The impact of it has stayed with me to this day. I had served the church for many years before that, but I'm not sure that I had loved the church all that much. Like most pastors I had carried the emotional scars from some bruising encounters with difficult parishioners over the years. Learning to love the church has made all the difference to my ministry. As I've reflected on that experience I think I begin to understand why it was so powerful. Behind the words of Bill Hybels I was really hearing the voice of Jesus, who loves the church, who longs to work through it, and who will never give up on it.
(Charles)

A church for our time

Our English word 'church' translates the Hebrew qahal in the Old Testament and the Greek ecclesia in the New Testament. Neither word refers to a settled group of people meeting just for worship on a regular basis. Qahal comes from a root meaning 'to call' and originally referred to the assembling of God's people for the purpose of hearing the law or sharing counsel. It could also be used to describe a mustering of the men of Israel to wage war. Ecclesia was an equally active word, used in secular Greek to denote the assembly of male citizens over the age of thirty who would meet to debate and decide on issues of the day.

It's significant that both qahal and ecclesia originally designated companies of people who met not merely for their own satisfaction, but to serve a greater cause and to enrich a wider community. That remains true about the ecclesia of Jesus Christ. Archbishop William Temple is famously reputed to have described the church as 'the only society on earth that exists for the benefit of non-members'. Like Israel of old, the church is called to be a 'kingdom of priests and a holy nation' (Exodus 19:6), chosen to be a blessing to every other nation, called to demonstrate the loving rule of God to all peoples on earth, and commissioned to bring the good news of God's salvation for his entire creation. Three things will characterize a church that learns to live for others in our time.

Telling out the story

If we go back to Peter's discourse on the Day of Pentecost (Acts 2:14–41) – the first Christian sermon ever preached – what do we find? Quite simply, he told a story to explain what had happened to his fellow disciples that was causing them to sound their praises in such an abandoned manner. They were not inebriated, as some of the more cynical onlookers had assumed. It was only 9 o'clock in the morning, much too early for a devout Jew to have indulged in his favourite tipple, even on a festival day! Their exuberance had come not from wine poured into a cup, but from the Spirit who had been poured into their hearts.

That in turn took him to the *Big Story* that made sense not just of what was happening on that day, but of life itself. It was a story that was rooted in the history of God's dealings with his people Israel – the part of the story that Peter's Jewish audience knew well. But it was a story whose purpose had been fulfilled in Jesus from Nazareth. His death had been more than a travesty of justice. It had been God's way of forgiving sin and healing his broken creation. God had been active in Jesus' death, God had brought him to life, and God was now pouring out his Holy Spirit so that the risen Jesus would be everywhere present with his people. The story obviously came with conviction and the hearers were 'cut to the heart' and began to ask, 'What shall we do?' Before the end of that day three thousand people responded and were added to the church.

Peter's story is our story, the story the world needs to hear. We need to tell it in all the 'languages' of our day – the spoken word, the visual image, the popular music that forms the soundtrack to our age. But there's something we mustn't miss if we want to tell the story convincingly. The initial impetus for Peter telling the story was to give the onlookers an *explanation* for the *demonstration* of the Holy Spirit's energy they had just witnessed among the believers. The story was *believable* not just because it was true, but because what was happening in the lives of Peter and others made it *credible*. There just had to be some good reason for what was happening, some proper explanation for why these people were different. And what happened on the Day of Pentecost was that three thousand people were so impressed by the demonstration of the Spirit's power and the explanation Peter gave that they said, 'We want what they're having!'

We moved into a fairly typical new estate nearly three years ago. Probably less than 10% of people have any real links with the church. So I have a very simple strategy for sharing my faith. I make it my aim to be the neighbour that everyone knows and trusts. I'm involved in HomeWatch and I'm part of a group who've organized a couple of street parties that have helped bring everyone together and create a sense of community. I try to walk round the estate a couple of times a week praying (with my eyes open!) and chatting to people.

I don't run an Alpha group or anything formal like that, though maybe that'll happen in time. But, as people ask questions or raise issues, I just try to respond as a follower of Jesus. In fact, I'm often more comfortable describing myself as a follower of Jesus rather than announcing that I'm a Christian. People have some really strange notions about Christianity and I find it easier to talk about

Jesus than try to straighten out all their opinions about organized religion.

I've found a very simple way of telling at least part of the story of Jesus. Every Christmas we have 'Neighbourhood Carols'. This year about fifty of our neighbours gathered in our driveway. We sang carols, read the Christmas story from Luke's Gospel, ate mince pies and drank coffee and mulled wine. It's funny, but if I said to my neighbours at any other time of the year, 'Would you like to come and stand outside our house in bitterly cold weather, sing some hymns and listen to a bit from the Bible?' they'd think I was crazy. But Christmas is different. It's a great chance to tell the story.

(Margaret)

Reaching out to our neighbours

If we want people to listen to the good news we have to share, then we need to *be* good news. Our lives must give as much evidence of being filled with the Spirit of God as did those of Peter and the other disciples at Pentecost. But we live at a time and in a culture that's very different from that of the first century AD. Church attendance has long been in decline in Britain. Unlike those Jews who gathered in Jerusalem from across the ancient world, our neighbours no longer flock to places of worship, even on the great religious festivals.

Yet the promise of Jesus to pour out his Spirit on his disciples remains ours. The challenge for us is to become sensitive to what I like to call 'Pentecost spaces' – moments and times when, in the midst of our everyday activities, people around us become aware of something more than the ordinary, something of the presence and power of God. Sometimes they'll be moments of great joy – the birth of a baby, listening to a moving piece of music, gazing at some breathtaking sight in the natural world.

At other times they'll be moments of deep sadness – the funeral of a family member, the break-up of a relationship, the end of a significant chapter in life. Sometimes they'll simply be those unexpected moments when everyone present is aware that there is far more to life than material prosperity and financial security. But it's at moments like these, if our lives are marked by authenticity and integrity as followers of Jesus, that people will turn to us and ask, just as they did at Pentecost, 'What does this mean? What should we do?' We won't need to answer them with a carefully crafted sermon or present them with a theological dossier. We'll just need to tell the story of Jesus and how our life has become part of that story, how it makes sense of life for us like nothing else has ever done or ever will do, and how they too can be part of the story.

Sending out disciples

Since most Christians will necessarily spend most of their time away from specifically church-based activities – looking after their families, earning a living, following legitimate leisure pursuits – that's where their discipleship needs to be expressed. It's the 'whole-life discipleship' we mentioned in chapter 6. We made the point then that the task of the church is not simply to recruit and retain members, but to resource and release disciples. That releasing mustn't be done grudgingly, regretting the fact that every hour they spend out in the world is an hour less they can be engaged in church activities. We need to *release* and *rejoice*! We need to *celebrate* as we deliberately and willingly *send* people out into the world.

Churches often hold commissioning services for those who are leaving for overseas missionary service. Congregations gladly receive reports of the challenges these missionaries are facing and the opportunities they're grasping to share the gospel. Intercessors gladly accept the responsibility of praying for 'those on the mission field'. *We need to be just as intentional about those who serve God right here, Monday to Friday, in the mission field of the school, the factory or the hospital.* We need to commission them all – Geoff the taxi-driver, Liz the cleaner, Bill the doctor, Helen the full-time homemaker and mum, Tom whose mission field includes hours spent at the job centre looking for work every week, Bob the grandfather who looks after his daughter's kids when she's at work. They're all disciples. They're all missionaries. Between them they're touching thousands of lives every week and they'll all be in places where no ordained priest or full-time pastor has been in years.

To imagine that they're only 'doing church' when they're attending a prayer meeting or helping with the parent-and-toddler club is to miss out on the true glory of the church. The glory of the church is that, if we'll only realize it, it cannot and must not be confined to Sunday worship and whatever else happens in the church building. The greater part of the ministry lies with Geoff, Liz, Bill, Helen, Tom, Bob and all the others: they *are* the church every day in the place where they work and the street where they live.

I'm suggesting a new benediction at the conclusion of all services – something like this: 'Brothers and sisters in Christ, we love you all. But if being a disciple is only about what you do in church, we've failed. So go on, get out there and get on with it! Be a whole-life disciple. Don't forget we'll all be praying for you. And when we meet up again next week and hear about the good things God's doing through you, we'll have a party. May the grace of our Lord Jesus Christ be with you all. Amen.'

Going Deeper

1. Here's a suggestion for one way in which we can support each other over the course of a month in the practice of whole-life discipleship. The group should be no larger than four to six people and should stick to one topic each week. For example:

   - Week 1: Family
   - Week 2: Work
   - Week 3: Church
   - Week 4: Leisure

   One by one, each person in the group has a maximum of five minutes to share their challenges and opportunities as disciples of Jesus in the area of life being considered that week. While each person is speaking no-one should interrupt, and after they've finished speaking everyone should be quiet for a minute or so to give space for God to speak. Then together the group should devote ten minutes to (a) highlighting any relevant and helpful passages of the Bible; (b) offering any brief advice and encouragement that seems appropriate; (c) praying for the person who has spoken and for the issues they have shared. There should be a moment of stillness again before moving on to the next person.

   It's important to keep in mind that the purpose is not in-depth counselling but mutual encouragement, and that whatever is shared must be regarded as confidential to the group.

2. How would you answer a non-Christian friend who asked you to explain why the church is important?

3. Despite a long decline in church attendance, in most towns and cities there is an almost bewildering variety of different

churches. Often you can find two or three churches on the same street within a few hundred yards of each other. How much does this help and how much does it hinder us in sharing the gospel with others?

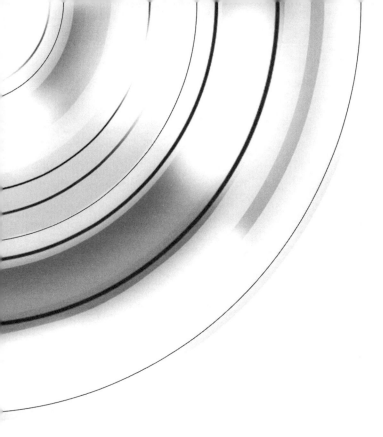

Engaging with the culture of the times

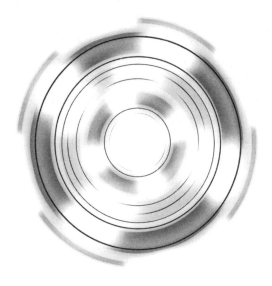

9. Engaging intelligently

Unprecedented upheaval

Just a few minutes before 5 o'clock in the evening on Tuesday 12 January 2010, two great tectonic plates on either side of the Enriquillo-Plantain Garden Fault shifted in opposite directions. This seismic activity resulted in an earthquake measuring 7.0 on the Richter Scale which wreaked death and destruction on the Caribbean country of Haiti. Buildings collapsed, thousands were instantly killed or were trapped beneath the rubble, and millions were made homeless. The scenes of suffering that filled our television screens in the following days were unbearably painful to witness. The experts told us that there were three things that made this tremor so destructive. First, it was centred just 10 miles south-west of the capital city, Port-au-Prince. Second, the quake was shallow – no more than 6 or 9 miles below the surface of the land. But the third and most important factor contributing to the resulting devastation was the fact that most homes and buildings in this desperately poor country were simply not built to a standard that would have enabled them to withstand the force of an earthquake of such magnitude.

For some five years I lived just outside Los Angeles in Southern California, another of the world's earthquake zones. We were fortunate in experiencing only a couple of minor tremors in our time there. Had we been around when some much bigger upheaval had taken place, I've no doubt that it would have been a very different experience. But it would in all probability have been far less destructive in terms of loss of life than the Haiti disaster. California's economy is, of course, much more affluent than that of Haiti. Consequently, over recent years, it has been able to invest significant sums of money in the twin strategies of earthquake preparedness and earthquake education. A programme has been put in place to reinforce buildings and bridges. Residents have been carefully instructed in simple procedures. Everyone, if they're sensible, keeps bottled water, basic food supplies and a well-stocked first aid kit at home and in the car. It's an indictment on the inequality of our world that thousands of Haitians perished for the want of such basic things.

We live in a time of unprecedented changes. It's not an inappropriate analogy to suggest that our society is experiencing an upheaval that's the moral and social equivalent of the seismic activity that all too often devastates unprepared and ill-equipped communities in developing countries. As we walk in the company of Jesus, we must do so through a cultural landscape that seems to be constantly shifting beneath our feet. Just as in the physical earthquake zones of this world, we need those twin strategies of being educated and prepared if we're to understand and engage effectively with our culture. To that end, it will help us to identify three areas where great 'tectonic plates' push against each other to produce some of the unsettling and unexpected convulsions that often seem to threaten the well-being and even the survival of our society.

Unresolved opposites

Secularization and spirituality

We're constantly reminded of the ongoing and seemingly irresistible process of secularization. Our society is either antagonistic towards religion or, as is more often the case, simply indifferent to it. The long centuries of European history in which the church possessed political power and held sway over many areas of life are swiftly drawing to a close. Church attendance in the UK continues its steady spiralling decline. God may not yet be dead philosophically for most of our contemporaries, but practically he's like the aged relative who's been consigned to the care of those who are skilled in theological geriatrics. Everyone else is content to pay him a prayerful visit at times of personal crisis or national catastrophe.

And yet, that's only half the truth. The demise of religion has been confidently predicted by futurists for decades, but religion is taking an unconscionably long time to die. National surveys conducted by independent bodies consistently reveal a deep-seated religious longing that refuses to be quenched by the onward march of secularization. Institutional religion may have been relegated to the margins by the majority of our neighbours, but 'spirituality' is definitely high on their agenda. A respected newspaper like *The Times* includes a section in its Saturday edition entitled 'Body & Soul' which gives space each week to some aspect of what they often call 'the spiritual dimension' of life. Secularization and spirituality may tug in opposite directions, but neither shows any sign of eliminating the other. The resulting upheaval is a mixture of high confusion and deep dissatisfaction that leads people to seek meaning in fringe cults and strange belief systems while ignoring the church at the end of their road.

Science and superstition

You can hear the assertions of militant atheists like Richard Dawkins that science provides the only real and reliable explanations for life repeated on just about any evening in your local pub with equal vehemence and conviction. 'Science', someone will confidently announce while ordering another pint, 'proves there's no God.' But half an hour later – without any sense of contradiction – the same drinker at the same bar will repeat his lucky mantra before buying his lottery ticket or touch his St Christopher medallion before setting off on his journey home. Superstition is all around us. Horoscopes feature in every popular newspaper, football managers wear the same lucky tie to sustain a winning streak, and palm-readers are still part of the entertainment scene in every seaside town. The popular trust in 'science' seems to be in direct contradiction to the persistent dependence on irrational superstitious practices. But in twenty-first-century Britain they continue to coexist – and ironically, in an age that rejects traditional religious faith, they are both examples of the willingness of millions to trust in things that they personally are unable to prove.

Modernity and postmodernity

We're often told – and not without good reason – that we live in postmodernity. Postmodern thinking is, to a considerable extent, a consequence of the fact that, as the twentieth century unfolded, it became clear that science and technology brought as many problems as they solved. Confronted with the threat of nuclear and biological warfare, the horrors of pollution and even the prospect of our planet's extinction, it became all but impossible to avoid the stark truth that human reason alone is unable to deliver the utopia that many had thought possible. Rationalistic materialism and faith in the inevitable progress of humanity were untenable in the face of the gas chambers of Auschwitz and the destruction of Hiroshima.

Postmodernity is a slippery concept, not easy to pin down, but there are some overriding characteristics that can be identified. The universe is seen not as a vast machine to be utilized for our purposes, but as an organic whole, a great cosmic process that needs to be treated with care. Human reason is no longer the certain route to all truth. Human beings, we're constantly reminded, are incapable of grasping an absolute and objective truth that's applicable to every place and every person. All we can hope for is a personal truth which will always be partial at best. The idea of a 'metanarrative', a big overarching story that explains the meaning and purpose of life, is discarded. Each person needs to create his or her own meaning through his or her own unique experiences.

Again, however, this isn't the whole picture. Modernity – the mindset and worldview that prevailed in Europe for five hundred years, that led to the great scientific discoveries of the Enlightenment, that made the Industrial Revolution possible, and that created the modern technological world in which we live and which we take for granted – is still very much with us. Academics may well debate and even doubt the validity of human reason, but they do so in centrally heated buildings, illuminated by electric light, with their laptops in front of them as they sip their espresso coffees. These are all the fruits of modernity, the products of rational thinking and empirical investigation. What's more, they may well send their children to schools that they've chosen because of their position in the league tables dedicated to charting academic success. Modernity and cold rationality are far from dead and they exist cheek by jowl with the uncertainties of postmodern thinking.

Unsettling changes

Like two great tectonic plates, these seemingly conflicting realities are constantly shifting and moving up against each other. And just like their geological equivalents, they inevitably produce intense activity and unprecedented convulsions in the moral, spiritual and social landscape. Consider some of the changes taking place in our culture.

I'm seventy-two now and I seem to have spent my life wishing there could be some credible spiritual dimension to my existence. My thoughts go round in the same circle, blocked at each rotation by the feeling that the divine mysteries are so mysterious that they're not compatible with plain common sense. Faith or reason? Do they have to be mutually exclusive? What can I do in my search for truth? Must I conclude with the French philosopher Pascal that 'the heart has its reasons that Reason doesn't know'?

A few years ago I asked my brother, 'What are we going to do about The Religious Bit?'

He just said, 'The whole thing's a conundrum. All you can do is to try to live as a considerate person.'

I was heartened recently when I turned on the radio just in time to hear of a man who asked a nun how he could find God. She replied with a smile, 'If you hadn't already found him, you wouldn't be looking for him.' Maybe I'm on board after all!

(Brian)

From significance to success

Just before writing this paragraph I glanced at a photo feature in the magazine section of a Sunday newspaper. It was a collection of photographs of little girls whose parents enter them in children's beauty pageants. The most disturbing one of all was of a two-year-old, professionally made up and elaborately coiffured, striking a pose for the camera. She's apparently already a veteran of the child beauty pageant circuit. Despite concerns for the impact all this might have on a child's self-esteem and for the fact that the shows might well be a target for paedophiles, the industry continues to flourish. It's just one extreme example of a culture in which the significance of simply being human has been traded for the success of becoming the best. We see it in undue pressure on teenagers to succeed at school, in the demands placed on employees to spend more time in the workplace than with their families, and in the push to be constantly 'upwardly mobile' that drives people into debt and depression. It's a far cry from the biblical view of human beings where what matters is our significance as creatures lovingly made in God's image, not our success as contestants scrabbling for first place in the rat-race of life.

From authority to celebrity

When winning is the ultimate goal, then what counts is to find the fast track that leads to success and to enjoy the trappings that follow from it. In an era of mass communication, our society has concluded that both are found in fame. A generation or so ago, our parents and grandparents admired the authority figures – members of parliament, police officers, doctors, teachers and the like. Today a prevailing cynicism has eroded respect for that kind of authority. Now we're obsessed with celebrity. We spend millions on magazines that give us glimpses into their extravagant lifestyles, we copy their fashions, and we create reality TV shows that give us – or at least people just like us – the chance to have our fifteen minutes of fame. Being recognized by others, we imagine, will provide us with a sense of identity and an assurance of success. Alas, it's a great delusion. On the one hand, it leads us to ignore the worth and work of those whose unsung service and personal sacrifice actually contribute most to the well-being of our society. On the other hand, the few who achieve fame often discover it to be an empty and unsatisfying substitute for real relationships and genuine intimacy with others.

From joiners to jugglers

An older generation grew up in a world in which most people spent a lifetime working at the same job, living in the same house, relating to the same group of friends, going to the same place on holiday every year, and attending the same church. Loyalty was inevitably high on the list of qualities they valued. In this age, life is very different. When opposite and competing ideas exist alongside one another, when things change rapidly, when people live busy lives, then they're much more reluctant to make lifelong commitments. Instead of joining, they juggle – they try different things, stick with them for as long as they find them meaningful, and then they move on. Of course, they may still take out membership of something that takes their interest, like the local gym, but as every gym in the country is aware, membership is not commitment. The trick is to get people to pay an annual membership fee in advance. The fact that hardly anyone who pays up will continue to come every week for an entire year means that you can enlist far more members than would be possible if they all turned up regularly. People with too many plates to spin and too many balls to keep in the air don't worry too much when they're forced to drop something.

We were chatting after church on Sunday morning when the conversation suddenly got very heated. Jean mentioned a programme she's been watching on TV. Our friend Bill reacted very strongly. He said he couldn't believe that a Christian would actually watch something with such bad language. I tried to explain that, while we didn't approve of the swearing on the programme, we did think it was good drama and a genuine attempt to look at some of the serious topics facing us today. But Bill wasn't having any of that and he gave us a hard time about it.

Bill's a great friend and I'm genuinely sorry that we've upset him. But I've been thinking a lot about our conversation and about the issues it raised. I guess we've all got two choices. Either we draw a very firm line and we don't watch anything that doesn't match up to our Christian standards, or we accept that some of the stuff we watch falls short of our principles and accept the challenge to think through where we stand on it. The danger with the first way is that you could easily get out of touch with the culture we've got to live in. The danger with the other way is that you kind of get sucked in and end up losing your Christian perspective completely. I wish there was a simple answer to it, but I think we're just going to have to accept the fact that we're in a sort of morally alien culture and we have to live with it.
(Frank)

From co-workers to consumers

When Britain was an agricultural economy we were, of necessity, co-workers. Whether you laboured on the land, ran the village shop, toiled in the smithy or helped transport the crop to the nearest market with your horse and cart, you shared the work and the produce. With the advent of the Industrial Revolution that close relationship changed. The move from small rural communities to living in cities combined with the growth of mass production meant that people became customers rather than co-workers, using their wages to purchase what they needed. Now life has moved on even from that. Modern technology and increased affluence mean that for a couple of generations we've lived with the assumption that it's our right to expect a constantly improving standard of material prosperity and an ever-increasing choice of goods. *The customer is no more; long live the consumer!* If we're unsure about our true identity, our society has largely concluded, we might be able to define who we are by the number of things we possess and the prestige of the brand names attached to them.

In the affluent West, consumerism has reached the point where it's become our religion: possessions have become our god, marketing has become our liturgy, shopping malls have become our temples, advertising jingles have become our hymns, the logos of the multinational companies have become our icons, designer clothes have become our vestments, obscenely wealthy celebrities have become the saints we venerate, and unlimited purchasing power has become the heaven of which we dream. No wonder it's been called *theo-capitalism*. Sadly, it's a belief system and a way of life that fails to deliver what it promises and leaves us emptier and more unfulfilled than before.

From ethics to aesthetics

Unsurprisingly, in a culture where people have lost a sense of personal significance, the basic question has begun to shift. If I can't find the answer to who I am, maybe I should settle for asking, 'Who can I become?' In earlier centuries, sincere seekers might have sought the answer in pursuing moral and spiritual progress, in becoming a better person, but popular interpretations of Freudian psychology and evolutionary philosophy have led many to abandon that path. If I'm no more than a sophisticated animal, if I'm not really making moral choices but simply being driven by deep inner drives from my subconscious, there's little point in the quest for ethical improvement. And if I can't change my inner person for the better, I can at least transform my outward appearance. *Farewell ethics; welcome aesthetics!* This is the age of cosmetic dentistry, plastic surgery and the pursuit of the perfect body. Find yourself a style guru and a personal trainer, and reach for eternal youth.

However, as in Jesus' story of the rich fool who thought only of himself and his personal well-being, reality and mortality have an uncomfortable habit of breaking through the false security of such self-obsession. For every man or woman the moment comes when 'your life will be demanded from you' (Luke 12:20). Sooner or later, the truth has to be faced that how you look is no substitute for how you live; outward appearance matters nothing compared to the ultimate purpose of loving God and loving our neighbour.

From consequences to options
My computer is smarter than I am! Whenever I want to delete a document, it double-checks that I really want to lose it. When I've hit the delete button, I can still go into the list of deleted documents and retrieve it. Even after that, IT boffins can recover stuff that I thought was long ago lost in cyberspace. More than once I've been rescued from what I thought were the irreversible consequences of my ineptitude at the keyboard. The virtual world of digital technology is one of options rather than strict consequences.

That same kind of thinking has permeated the real world of everyday living – the world in which we make decisions and moral choices. Parents and community leaders used to caution younger people against careless sexual behaviour by warning them of the consequences of sexually transmitted diseases or unwanted pregnancy. Lifelong heterosexual marriage was widely regarded as 'the right thing' to do, even if many failed to adhere to that counsel. Divorce and broken families were seen as serious consequences to be avoided. Now, however, we live in a society in which the emphasis is much more on assessing the options rather than weighing up the consequences. The question 'Is this right?' has been replaced by questions like 'How does it feel?', 'Can I do this without hurting others?' and 'Is this the best option for everyone concerned?' Hard moral decisions, especially in the area of human sexuality, have been replaced by personal lifestyle options.

From principles to people

Very often Christians view this way of thinking as a complete loss of morality. It's certainly a seismic shift in how people view right and wrong. The moral landscape has been rearranged. It's certainly not all for the better and it's a very dangerous ground to traverse, but what makes it so tricky for the disciple who wants to walk with Jesus is that in all this moral upheaval there may be both positive and negative things beginning to emerge. Only if we hold true to the gospel and only if we understand our culture will we find some solid ground beneath our feet.

Let me offer an illustration of the complexity of what's happening. In 2004 the football pundit Ron Atkinson had just finished his post-match analysis of a game involving Chelsea Football Club. Believing the broadcast was over, he made a remark about one of the Chelsea players. Atkinson's previous record as a football manager – he was among the first to select black players for his teams – would strongly suggest that he isn't a racist. But on that evening his words had unpleasant racist overtones when he described Marcel Desailly as a 'f----- lazy thick n-----'. Unfortunately, a technician had failed to turn off the microphones and Atkinson's ill-advised comments were heard in parts of the Middle East.

In the resulting furore Atkinson was forced to offer his resignation and the television company had no alternative but to accept it. There was, however, something very interesting about it all that went largely unnoticed. Forty years ago Atkinson would have lost his job because of his use of the F-word. In those days the nation had principles about the use of obscene language. But in all the comments that followed the incident, hardly anyone seemed to notice that word. What cost Atkinson his job was the N-word, his insulting and stereotypical description of a fellow human being. It was a perfect example of *the change from a concern for principles to a compassion for people.* Most Christians would have been deeply offended by Atkinson's swearing, but for almost everyone else it was far less significant than the racial and personal slur on a young man who was generally respected. The question for us as Christians is this: in our proper concern for moral principles, have we sometimes forgotten that Jesus was always more concerned about showing love to ordinary people than about observing the legal niceties of a moral code?

There will be a constant challenge for us, as followers of Jesus, to discern what is good and to do what is right. There are moral standards that we must uphold. But there is an even greater challenge and a greater opportunity. We live in a world that is fallen and confused, but in which the Spirit of God continues to move and touch hearts and lives. Our non-Christian neighbours are sometimes able to glimpse and grasp aspects of God's truth that we can too easily forget. One of those aspects is that God is defined by love, not by laws. That may well provide us with the opportunity to demonstrate by our lives the good news that God loves his broken world and longs to heal it.

Going Deeper

1. In recent years some Christians have forbidden their children to read the Harry Potter books on the grounds that they are un-Christian. Others have called on their fellow believers to boycott the movie *The Golden Compass*, based on the first book in Philip Pullman's *His Dark Materials* trilogy. How can we best respond to films and novels which don't reflect our Christian worldview?

2. Here are four statements to discuss with a group of fellow disciples:

   a) Popular culture in our country is a godless zone.
   b) Sometimes people who are not Christians discern the truth on some of the big issues of life more clearly than the church does.
   c) Moral standards in Britain have deteriorated in every area of life over the last thirty years.
   d) True disciples of Jesus should give away everything they own apart from what is absolutely necessary to live on.

3. There is a great deal of criticism of the 'politically correct' culture in which we live. Here are some comments by Mark Greene. Is he right?

   Both the gospel and PC culture share a common desire for right relationships. So the key to freedom in speech and to negotiating the PC world minefield is the ability to develop dynamic, trusting relationships where we do not seek power over others, where we serve their interests and where they trust us to do so. The antidote to PC world is to exercise the central tenet of JC world.[1]

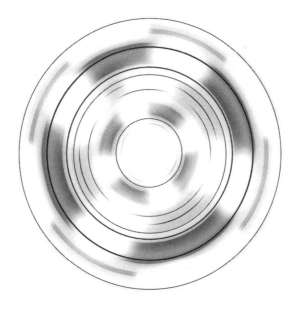

10. Engaging Christianly

Sturdy crafts or supple fish

Frederick Otis Barton Jr was an American deep-sea diver and inventor with a passion to explore the depths of the ocean. To fulfil his ambition he designed the bathysphere, an unpowered submersible made from thick cast steel. The vessel was lowered into the sea suspended from a cable and linked to the surface by a rubber hose that carried an electrical supply and a telephone connection. In June 1934 he took his strange-looking spherical craft to a depth of over 3,000 feet. His bathysphere had allowed him to engage with the ocean environment in a way that had not been possible before.

Nonetheless, Barton must have been aware of an irony as he gazed through the 3-inch-thick windows at the wonders of the ocean outside. His craft weighed 10,000 pounds, making the cable linking him to the surface unmanageable at extreme depths – but the fish that he was observing were swimming around him free from the clumsy limitations of the heavy bathysphere. The difference was simply that they were able to withstand the pressure of the ocean depths not because of a thick protective skin, but by virtue of an equal and opposite inner force.

Too often Christians imagine that the only way to deal with our culture is to live in a kind of spiritual bathysphere from which we can safely observe and critique society without becoming engulfed. The truth is that the fish provide a much better example. When Paul wrote his letter to the Romans, he was mindful of the fact that this little group of disciples was seeking to follow Jesus right at the heart of the political, military and cultural centre of the empire. The J. B. Phillips translation captures Paul's meaning perfectly and powerfully as he counsels his readers on how to live Christianly in an alien and confusing culture: 'Don't let the world around you squeeze you into its own mould, but let God re-mould your minds from within, so that you may prove in practice that the plan of God for you is good, meets all his demands and moves towards the goal of true maturity' (Romans 12:1–2, JBP). There's no escaping the fact: unless our characters and our values are shaped by the teaching of Jesus and the power of his Spirit from within, they will inevitably be shaped and moulded by the constant pressure of the prevailing culture in which we live. The question is this: How can we put ourselves in the place where God can 're-mould [our] minds from within', and what kind of people do we need to be to engage Christianly and meaningfully with the culture of our times?

Seeking deep spirituality

Neither a dry doctrinal orthodoxy nor a frenetic well-intentioned activism will be adequate as we seek to connect with our culture. We need to become spiritually deep people whose engagement with the world flows out of a prior and greater engagement with God. That's one reason why so many are rediscovering and reclaiming the great classic spiritual disciplines. They're neither attempts to gain God's favour, nor efforts at self-improvement. Instead, they're the way in which we cooperate with God and intentionally enrol in his school for disciples, allowing his Holy Spirit to inform our thinking and transform our living so that we begin the lifelong process of becoming more and more like Jesus. Here are just four spiritual disciplines to consider.

Prayer

Of course, prayer is central – deliberately making time and space to listen to God and to communicate our hopes, fears and deepest desires. One of the most encouraging moments in the Gospels occurs when the disciples go to Jesus and say, 'Lord, teach us to pray' (Luke 11:1). It frees us from the fear that we have to be perfect at praying. It tells us that prayer is something we *can* learn to do better. And, best of all, Jesus gives us a brief prayer on which we can model our own prayers. It's a prayer that addresses God as Father, that gives him the honour he deserves, that prays for his kingly rule to be established, that asks for our daily needs to be supplied, that recognizes our need to give and receive forgiveness, that seeks God's protection from evil and ends by ascribing to him all the authority that's rightly his. That, as they say, is a prayer that ticks all the boxes.

I became a Christian as a teenager, and something real happened in my life that night. I linked up with a lively church where there was good Bible teaching and uplifting worship and I made some great friends. I'm still part of that church.

But as the years have passed, there's something that's troubled me. For a long time I thought that my spiritual growth would be automatic. You know the kind of teaching, 'You don't need to struggle or strive, just say "Yes" to the Holy Spirit and you'll grow more like Jesus.' But it didn't happen for me like that. After the first flush of enthusiasm, I just seemed to get stuck for a long time.

The last couple of years have been different. In conversation one evening we discovered that a whole group of us were feeling pretty much the same. John shared some stuff he'd been reading on intentionally following a course of spiritual disciplines. It sounded challenging but also exciting. The upshot was that we committed to follow through on this together. So we meet twice a month. It's not just another Bible study group. It's much more intentional than that, much more about learning how to live, and we hold each other accountable for our progress.

It's a bit like when I was training to run a half-marathon. The training didn't turn me into an Olympic gold medallist, but I slowly got better and stronger. Well, I'm not up there with Mother Teresa yet, but I think that little by little I'm growing more Christ-like.

(Lucy)

Meditation

Meditation is a lot more 'normal' and accessible than we often think. It's a close cousin of prayer itself. Experienced teachers in the art of meditation will often talk of the need to 'centre down', to slow the breathing, to release feelings of anger or tension and to relax the body, in order that we can begin to reflect on some deep truth. It might be a sentence from Scripture, an incident in the Gospels, a scene from nature or an image of the cross – or a thousand other things on which your attention can be focused. The point is *not* that *you work out* what it means. The point is to *let it work in you*. Meditation isn't irrational, but it acts at a deeper level than the purely rational mind, engaging the imagination and reaching deep into your heart and spirit.

Study

If meditation refreshes our spirits, then study renews our minds. Meditation touches us to the depths of our hearts; study transforms what goes on in our heads. Both are equally important. The most effective followers of Jesus have warm hearts and cool heads. Study involves the obvious task of reading the Bible in a way that asks the important and relevant questions: What does this scripture mean? What does it mean for us today? How should we live in the light of this particular truth, and what needs to change?

This is more than just 'Bible study'. All truth is God's truth. Pious platitudes and well-meaning but ill-thought-through responses to difficult questions will not do. We need men and women who will study in all kinds of academic disciplines in order to become informed disciples in every walk of life – politicians and police officers, lawyers and labourers, teachers and tram-drivers – men and women whose minds are steeped in Scripture, who have mastered the skills and demands of their jobs and professions, who are seeking to think through the issues of our day.

Fasting

It's clear that Jesus took it for granted that fasting would be part of the life of his disciples (Matthew 6:16), and it was a significant part of the life and worship of the believers in Acts

(Acts 13:2). Throughout the history of the church, fasting has been regularly practised and is frequently mentioned in manuals of devotion. At times it has degenerated into asceticism or been hijacked by religious fanatics, but properly understood and practised, fasting belongs neither to legalists nor to a lunatic fringe. It belongs in the mainstream life of the church and can benefit every believer.

Fasting is about being liberated from the things that would keep us from God. It's often linked with times of intense worship and is intended to help us focus our whole attention on God. It has particular power at times of repentance, when we're seeking to discover God's heart on some matter, or when we're praying to be led by his Spirit and filled with his power. Fasting also works to uncover the truth about ourselves. It not only reveals just how much our life revolves around food, but it also exposes tensions and irritations that lie just under the surface. Eating often serves to cover up and stifle those things. Fasting brings us to a place where we recognize our needs and allow God to deal with them.

That, of course, is the purpose of all the spiritual disciplines – to mould us so that our characters are formed by the presence and power of the living Christ and not by the pressure of a changing culture; to make us who we were always meant to be because we've been liberated from the tyranny of self. When that inner transformation is taking place in us, then we have some real hope of demonstrating to a watching world the change that the gospel can effect in other people and in society at large.

Avoiding narrow piety

This inner spirituality, through which we're becoming ever more Christ-like, has to be the soil in which our personal integrity is rooted. Who we are, and what we are becoming, in

Christ must be reflected in how we live in the world. Regrettably, we've sometimes had a 'bathysphere' understanding of spirituality, looking out at the world but preoccupied with keeping ourselves safe from the external pressures of our culture. That results in a narrow and constricted view of spiritual maturity.

Personal morality

It can mean that we measure spiritual maturity primarily or even exclusively in terms of personal morality, particularly as it relates to sexual conduct. Of course, our personal moral standards are of the highest importance. When we ignore such things as honesty in financial matters and fidelity in marriage, we make a travesty of the gospel and a tragedy of our lives. *But they're not the whole picture* when it comes to being a follower of Jesus. In truth, it's possible to be beyond reproach in these areas and yet to be far short of what God wants us to be. The rich young ruler had kept the law meticulously, but his religion was entirely lacking in devotion to Jesus or compassion for the poor (Luke 18:18–25).

Church activity

Sometimes involvement in church activity is seen as the essential indicator of a person's spiritual temperature. Such involvement is undeniably important. A healthy Christian community needs people who will undertake the ministries that are necessary for the ongoing worship and witness of the congregation. But of itself *it's an unreliable indication of spiritual maturity*. It can even become a cover-up for a lack of genuine relationship with God. In Jesus' story of the lost son, the elder brother's seemingly exemplary conduct and faithful service merely served to conceal a harsh and bitter spirit that was very different from his father's forgiving heart (Luke 15:25–32). It's a syndrome that's not unknown among Christians today.

Group conformity

Although it's rarely articulated, churches can easily default to gauging the maturity of their members by how readily they conform to the culture of the group. There are churches where just mastering the right spiritual jargon will be taken as a sure sign of personal piety; where certain styles of dress will cause some to doubt your holiness; where participation in practices considered 'worldly' will put you outside the pale; where daring to express doubts about some distinctive denominational doctrinal nuance will make the faithful throw up their hands in horror. All that just serves to demonstrate that the exclusiveness of the Pharisees isn't confined to a Jewish sect in New Testament times. All of us who believe that the church is still intrinsic to God's strategy for his redemptive purposes need to guard against it.

Demonstrating generous integrity

A true disciple is someone who is making a whole-life response to Jesus and who is seeking to become more Christ-like in every aspect of life, the public as well the private and personal. *In our complex postmodern, post-Christendom society it is only that kind of discipleship that will have a lasting and transforming effect on our culture.* We'll achieve more by our distinctive presence than by strident protests; we'll have a greater impact on our neighbours by demonstrating an alternative and attractive lifestyle than by demanding that they accept absolute truths; and we'll gain a more attentive hearing for the gospel by a winsome Christ-like character than by winning a confrontation. How then should we live so that we embody the truth of the gospel?

Living simply and generously

Our culture judges the worth of people by three criteria – their beauty, their property and their celebrity. Its values of consumerism and individualism are in stark contrast to the teaching of Jesus: 'Watch out and guard yourselves from every kind of greed; because a person's true life is not made up of the things he owns, no matter how rich he may be' (Luke 12:15 GNB).

We must neither succumb to the pressure around us, nor take the way of asceticism and see all material things as evil. The secret is to see all possessions as gifts from a loving Creator and to recognize that they're given for us to enjoy but never to exploit. Our calling is to live simply. Our goal is to be grateful stewards of God's gifts, not greedily to stockpile the maximum amount of material goods. That should affect every area of our lives – the money we spend, the possessions we own, the homes we live in, the cars we drive, the amount of food we eat, the clothes we wear. Some might think it would be easier if Jesus had given a rigid rule about all these things, something that specified exactly how much we were allowed to have. But that would be legalism, and the gospel is all about liberty and the responsibility that goes with it to make our own decisions as men and women whose thinking is being renewed as we walk in the company of Jesus and live in the power of his Spirit.

Living simply frees us to live generously with a liberality that applies not just to our money and our possessions, but to every area of our life. We need to be generous with the time that we give to others, with the hospitality that we show when we open our homes, and with the service that we offer in the ministries to which we're called. Most of all, we demonstrate Christ-like generosity in our willingness to forgive. When his disciples asked him where the line should be drawn on forgiveness, Jesus gave them what was in cold logic a ridiculous answer. If the scribes and lawyers put a limit of seven times, Jesus multiplied that by seventy! In other words: stop counting, start forgiving, and break through the boundaries of legality into the extravagant expanse of generous love.

Living restfully and justly

The proper observance of the Sabbath was a constant source of controversy between Jesus and the Pharisees. They had turned it into a mass of rules and regulations, but he sought to restore it to its proper place as an opportunity for refreshment and renewal. 'The Sabbath was made for man, not man for the Sabbath,' he reminded them (Mark 2:27). Had they understood their Scriptures better, they would have realized that observing the Sabbath is an act of trust even more than an act of obedience. The Sabbath as a day of rest is grounded in the story of creation. The God who spoke the universe into existence is the God who has built the rhythm of work and rest into the very warp and woof of his creation. If he took time to rest, so should we. As the Israelites were to learn in their journey through the desert, the Sabbath was a time to rest in the knowledge that God who had set them free would take care of their needs. He would provide sufficient manna so that they could rest from collecting it for one day.

The Sabbath is also about justice. The fourth commandment didn't apply just to you. No-one was to work on the Sabbath – not you, not your children, not your servants, not even your livestock! Significantly, in a culture that regarded the foreigner as an enemy and an intruder, it also included 'the alien within your gates' (Exodus 20:8–11). The commandments were given first to a company of liberated slaves on their way to a homeland, and the Sabbath commandment gets right to the heart of how they were to use their new-found freedom. A society that cannot see beyond productivity and material prosperity, that sets wealth and work above everything else, is a ruthless as well as a restless society. The endless quest for more will always go hand in hand with the exploitation of the poor and underprivileged.

For disciples of Jesus, observing the Sabbath will include but go far beyond complying with a day of rest. We mustn't forget those key words in the commandment: it's to be 'a Sabbath to the LORD your God' (Exodus 20:10). It calls us to *reflect on*, and to *reflect to others* by our lives, the character of God who is both generous in his provision for our needs and righteous in his concern for justice. We are to live restfully, trusting his provision, taking time to enjoy his creation, and concerning ourselves for the poor and the marginalized in our world.

Live transformingly

I know, 'transformingly' isn't really a proper word! But it's the only one I can think of to convey my meaning. If what we've been saying in the last few chapters of this book is true, then you can't have missed the point. Pious withdrawal from the world isn't an option for disciples. It isn't even enough just to pray for the world. We've got to be *involved* in such a way that we begin to transform the world by our lives and our actions. The world needs disciples in every walk of life – police officers, postmen, politicians, porters, probation officers, philosophers, pharmacists . . . and any other profession you can think of! I love the story of the young man who, when asked his occupation, replied, 'I'm a disciple of Jesus disguised as a car mechanic.'

Our discipleship is meaningless if it isn't lived out every day of the week. Jesus told us to be salt and light. One does its work by unseen penetration, the other by obvious illumination. *Both have an effect just by being what they are.* Similarly, disciples should effect transformation just by being disciples. Evangelistic strategies won't change our world for the better. Discipleship programmes won't revolutionize our society. There's no undiscovered ecumenical agenda that will impact our society for God and for good. But there are millions of 'ordinary' followers of Jesus, men and women like you and me who spend our time with our families, our friends, our work colleagues and our neighbours. We are the ones who can and must get involved in every walk of life and live *transformingly*. We must live our lives, bring up our families, relate to our neighbours, cast our votes, do our jobs, work for justice, run for the local council, stand for parliament, take our place as school governors, share the good news about Jesus in word and deed – and do it all with an unquenchable joy and an unstoppable determination that will bring the transforming power of the gospel to every situation.

Going Deeper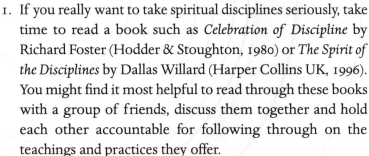

1. If you really want to take spiritual disciplines seriously, take time to read a book such as *Celebration of Discipline* by Richard Foster (Hodder & Stoughton, 1980) or *The Spirit of the Disciplines* by Dallas Willard (Harper Collins UK, 1996). You might find it most helpful to read through these books with a group of friends, discuss them together and hold each other accountable for following through on the teachings and practices they offer.

2. The Anglican Church worldwide has drawn up a practical 'checklist' for mission activities. They identify five key purposes for the church:

   - to proclaim the good news of the kingdom;
   - to teach, baptize and nurture new believers;
   - to respond to human need by loving service;
   - to seek to transform unjust structures of society;
   - to strive to safeguard the integrity of creation and sustain and renew the life of the earth.

   How well do you feel your church embodies these principles in its ministry? In what aspects can your church be more effective? What can you do as an individual to help this?

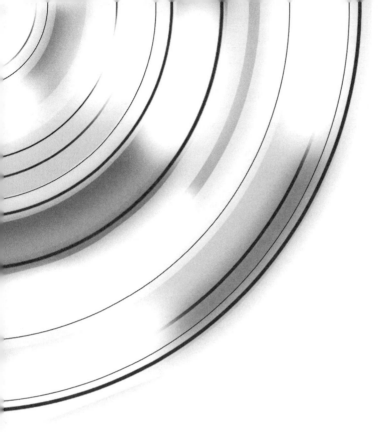

Looking to the
coming of the King

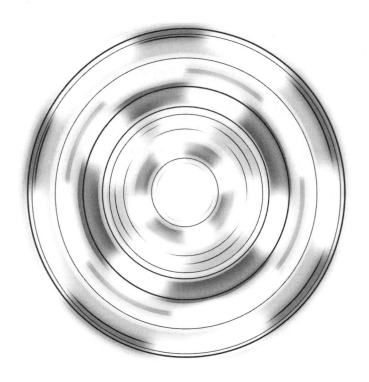

11. What will be, will be

The expectation of victory: changing the song

When Doris Day first sang '*Que Sera, Sera*' in a 1950s movie, the cinema audience could never have imagined how much the meaning of the song would change in half a century. Despite its jaunty tune, the lyrics are essentially fatalistic. The little girl who asks her mother if she'll grow up to be pretty and rich, and the young woman who asks her sweetheart what lies ahead and whether they can expect rainbows day after day, both receive the same answer. *Whatever will be, will be.* The future will unfold inexorably and unalterably, and there's absolutely nothing we can do about it.

Fast-forward fifty years, and the meaning of the song has been turned on its head. 'Que Sera, Sera' is sung at football matches all over the country by the fans of the winning team, particularly in the later rounds of the FA Cup when they anticipate the appearance of their heroes in the final at the national stadium in West London. With absolute conviction they raise their voices and sing over and over again (ad nauseam, some might say):

Que sera, sera – whatever will be, will be.
We're going to Wem-bi-lee!
Que sera, sera . . .

There's nothing fatalistic here. That little phrase, 'whatever will be, will be', has been transformed. Instead of expressing a resigned acceptance of an unknown and uncertain future, it has become the promise of an ultimate and certain victory. Their commitment to the cause, their support for the team and their confidence in the ability of the manager and players to deliver the success they crave has transformed passive pessimism into passionate optimism.

Disciples of Jesus can be infected by a fatalistic outlook without even realizing it. We can easily feel overwhelmed by the issues of our day – economic difficulties, environmental challenges, political tensions and military confrontations. Then there's the undeniable fact that for all of our lifetime the church in Britain and throughout Europe has been in numerical decline. Some Christians hold on stubbornly to the status quo, determined not to lose the little that they still have. Others give up on the church as a lost cause. Others still simply lapse from any active commitment to Jesus Christ. At best, the future's an uncertain prospect. At worst, it seems to promise only the continuing demise of the church and even the ultimate defeat of all we believe in.

Disciples, however, can learn lessons from all kinds of people – even football fans! *We too can sing a different song, a new song.* The despondent dirge that all too often seems to echo around the church can become a hymn of expectant praise for a future beyond our imaginings. Followers of Jesus have much more cause to turn a fatalistic ballad into a faith-filled anthem than the passionate hordes who file through the turnstiles at Old Trafford or Anfield. We're committed to the most important cause and to the greatest leader in all human history. If we're in the middle of a tough passage of play at this particular moment, that must never blind us to the fact that the momentum of the game is definitely going our way. But to appreciate that, we need to set our discipleship in the context of the 'end game' and look to the coming of the King.

The motivation of our efforts: the reign of God

Jesus declared that the long-awaited reign of his Father – the kingdom of God – had broken into the world. It was a declaration that threatened every power base and every other claim to rule. By his words and deeds, Jesus was announcing God's sovereign rule over *every* area of life and human affairs. When he healed the sick he was declaring it over disease and sickness. When he walked on the water he was declaring it over nature. When he challenged the teaching of the scribes and Pharisees he was declaring it over the spiritual and moral realm. When he forgave people he was declaring it over human sin. When he rode into Jerusalem on the back of a donkey under the very noses of the occupying Roman army, he was declaring that the authority his Father had entrusted to him was greater than that of Caesar.

Nonetheless, there's a tension at the heart of Jesus' teaching about the kingdom of God. On the one hand, the kingdom is here and now. God is already at work overcoming evil, putting things to rights and restoring the world to his original intention at creation. On the other hand, the kingdom is still to be fully established. This remains a fallen and imperfect world. Setbacks, sickness and sin are still very much with us, a fact Jesus acknowledges when he teaches his disciples to pray,

Your kingdom come,
your will be done
  on earth as it is in heaven.
(Matthew 6:10)

That's a prayer that challenges us to work and pray for a more perfect realization of God's kingdom in our midst; and since Jesus directs us to pray for it, it assures us that one day that prayer will be fully answered.

Sometimes we lose sight of the fact that God is at work building his kingdom in the here and now, and an *ungodly frustration* sets in. Discipleship becomes a weary struggle on a treadmill of exhausting effort. At other times Christians forget that the kingdom has still to come in all its fullness. That produces an impossible perfectionism, an unbalanced spirituality, and an *unbiblical presumption*. You hear it in misleading teaching that tells us that Christians needn't ever suffer from illness, that we can live completely sinless lives, or that we have an entitlement to be wealthy and free from any trials and tribulations in life.

By contrast, a true understanding of the kingdom of God leads us neither to an *ungodly frustration*, nor to an *unbiblical presumption*, but to an *eager and active expectation*. God *is* building his kingdom and one day that kingdom *will* come in all its fullness. Evil will be overcome by good, hate will be conquered by love, and every knee in heaven and on earth will bow and every tongue will confess that Jesus is Lord and King (Philippians 2:10–11). Until that day we continue to work, confident that God will use all our efforts to that great end. We know that every victory we win and every good we achieve in his name will be partial, imperfect and incomplete. But we also have an expectation that, in a way we cannot fully understand at this moment, our humble efforts will become part of God's perfect, completed work.

We were discussing natural disasters in the office the other week. Inevitably somebody raised the question of how a loving God can allow such things. They all looked at me, challenging me to make a response. I've long ago learned that there isn't a neat and easy answer to that question, certainly not the kind that would satisfy a room full of sceptics.

So I said that although I don't have all the answers, there are a couple of things I hold on to in this kind of situation. This is a dangerous world where bad things sometimes happen to innocent people. If they press me on that, I try to explain my understanding of this being a 'fallen world'. But the other thing that I try to emphasize s that I believe I see signs of God's love in the way people respond to these disasters – everything from the people who donate money for relief work to the people who risk their lives digging through the rubble trying to save others. I can't think why people would do stuff like that unless there's a loving God who inspires such selfless service. And if that's true, then it's just a small step for me to trust that a God like that will one day put everything to rights.

(Sam)

The foundation of our hope: the resurrection of Jesus

To believe in the coming kingdom of God in the face of sickness, injustice and tragedy is to be possessed of an audacious hope. Yet this isn't just a peculiarly religious strain of the age-old human malaise of looking for the pot of gold at the end of the rainbow. There *is* a firm foundation for our hope. It's built on the discovery of an empty tomb in a garden just outside Jerusalem two thousand years ago, and on the unforgettable events that followed. Some women among Jesus' little band of followers had gone to the tomb intending to perform some final service for the body of their crucified leader, but all they found was a heap of discarded grave-clothes. More important still were the encounters with the risen Jesus that followed in the ensuing days and weeks, encounters that left the disciples utterly convinced that he was alive.

It wasn't just that they thought he'd come back from the dead, that he'd been resuscitated like his friend Lazarus (John 11:38–44). No, they were convinced that they were witnessing something of an entirely different order. Jesus had not come back from the dead. He'd gone right through death and come out the other side. *He had conquered death.* It was the ultimate triumph of good over evil. This wasn't *resuscitation*; this was *resurrection*. This was a mighty act of God and it vindicated everything Jesus had said and done. But it was much more than that. Jesus really has been raised from the dead, becoming a *whole* person with a brand-new body, albeit one freed from the limitations of time and space. The implications are startling. It means that God *has* broken through. It means that on that first Easter Sunday God's will *has* been done on earth as in heaven. And, as Paul argues so convincingly, the resurrection of Jesus is a unique event only in its timing. What God has done for Jesus in the middle of history, he will one day do for us at the end of time. To be human is to be subject to death – but to be 'in Christ' is to share in his resurrection. Eugene Peterson paraphrases Paul's words in the colloquial English of our day: 'If all we get out of Christ is a little inspiration for a few short years, we're a pretty sorry lot. But the truth is that Christ *has* been raised up, the first in a long legacy of those who are going to leave the cemeteries' (1 Corinthians 15:18–20, *The Message*, italics original).

It doesn't stop there. If God will one day raise our bodies to life, then it follows that he's not merely concerned with the renewal of the spiritual realm. The resurrection carries the promise of the restoration of the entire physical and material universe. God's plan of salvation certainly includes the forgiveness of our sins and the raising of our bodies, but it also encompasses the ultimate redemption of the whole created order. We're not God's only concern, though we do have a central role to play in the working out of his grand strategy. Again, it's Paul who brings out the truth. Pain and suffering are part of the present reality, but they're as nothing compared to what awaits us. And when God completes his work in our lives, all creation will take its cue from us and share that transformation:

> I consider that our present sufferings are not worth comparing with the glory that will be revealed in us. The creation waits in eager expectation for the sons of God to be revealed. For the creation was subjected to frustration, not by its own choice, but by the will of the one who subjected it, in hope that the creation itself will be liberated from its bondage to decay and brought into the glorious freedom of the children of God. (Romans 8:18–21)

We inhabit a culture that lives just for the moment, demanding instant gratification. We see it in the rampant consumerism of our age and in the seeming inability of so many people to make lasting commitments and long-term relationships. Those are all signs of a deeper malaise. They point to the fact that this is a generation which has largely lost real hope for the future. The ever-present threat of terrorism, the possibility of global war and the prospect of environmental catastrophe conspire together to convince many of our contemporaries that the only option is to live as if there will be no tomorrow.

The challenge to disciples is to live 'resurrection lives' here and now. We're right to believe that the resurrection carries the promise of life *after* death, but we're wrong if we see it as being operative only beyond the grave. The resurrection of Jesus happened in our time and space, not in the far-off regions of eternity. It released God's power in the here and now, and it carries the promise of life *before* death. The whole creation will be renewed when God's children are revealed. That renewing and revealing needs to happen every day as we share the good news of Jesus, as we seek to be good neighbours and honest citizens, as we feed the hungry and care for the sick, and as we work at every level of society to make the world a more just place.

I remember watching Match of the Day *in January 2008 when Kevin Keegan stepped onto the pitch at St James's Park for his first home game since returning to manage his beloved Newcastle United. Fifty thousand Geordies went crazy. Most of them were wearing gold cardboard crowns with the words 'The return of King Kev' written on them. Sadly, the euphoria didn't last. Just eight months later, following a series of disappointing results, King Kev resigned his post and left.*

I told that story the other Sunday when I spoke about the second coming of Jesus. I told my people that I think I've been in danger of growing cynical and losing my sense of expectancy. I've seen so many false dawns over the years. If it's not a new initiative for evangelism, then it's a new programme for church growth. And I've heard so many high-profile speakers prophesying that revival is just around the corner. In reality, not a lot has changed.

But if our King is coming back, then it makes all the difference. It does matter what we do, even when we don't see immediate changes in the world or massive growth in the church. I'm going to preach on that topic again. If it didn't inspire the people in the pews, it certainly fired me up!
(Hugh)

The consummation of the kingdom: the return of the King

There are two mistakes that are made regarding the 'second coming' of Jesus. One is to read books of the Bible – such as Daniel and Revelation – like a railway timetable. They're part of a biblical genre known as 'apocalyptic'. The writers were concerned to encourage their readers living through difficult times by assuring them that God was in control and the future was assured. In order to grab the attention of their readers, they couched their message in vivid and surreal imagery. They certainly weren't primarily concerned with predicting precise dates that can be glibly matched up with the events of our day. Those who've tried to do that have been proved wrong far too often. It just isn't a helpful way to read the Bible.

The other error is to use these books to frighten people into accepting Jesus with dire warnings of what happens to unbelievers who are left behind while those of us who are Christians get caught up in the air and taken off to heaven with Jesus. In fact, what's called 'the Rapture' is really a misunderstanding based on a faulty reading of a passage in Paul's first letter to the Thessalonians (1 Thessalonians 4:13–18). Paul paints a vivid word-picture of Jesus coming 'in the clouds' and being met by the saints. What would have been in his mind was a custom in the ancient world. When the king came to visit one of the outposts of his kingdom, the citizens would go out to meet him as a mark of respect. They would then accompany him as he processed through the gates of their city. *They weren't about to go off with the king to his palace. He was coming to their city to take up residence.* So Paul's words about meeting Jesus 'in the air' are not intended to describe our *departure* with Jesus. They're certainly not meant as a warning to those who might get left behind. They're words of *encouragement* to believers. They're intended to encourage us to 'keep on keeping on', to live for Jesus here and now and to work to make this a better world. We can do so confident in the knowledge that Jesus will come again to usher in the new order, and that God's kingdom will be finally and perfectly established in our world.

Our calling is to live out this future reality in the present as citizens of the coming kingdom. We're to live by its values and trust in its promises, even when events seem to point in the opposite direction. As followers of Jesus, what kind of lives should we live? Why should we share the story of Jesus with non-believers? Why should we be concerned about the difficult ethical questions of our day – embryo experimentation, reproductive technology, euthanasia, nuclear weapons, and a host of other complex issues? What do we believe about environmental issues? What should we do about world poverty and hunger? In the end, how we respond to all of these questions will be governed by our belief that life does have meaning because Jesus is coming again and because God will renew his entire creation.

I used to think that there was a great moment in everybody's life when God revealed to them what he wanted them to do. I'm sure some people do have something like that, and that's really great for them. But the great moment for me was when I realized that there wasn't a 'great moment' and that my calling as a disciple was staring me in the face.

I've got a husband and three kids who need to see God's love in their mum. I work part time as a teaching assistant in a school where the teachers are stretched and under stress, and where loads of the kids come from broken and dysfunctional families. Sometimes my 'Christian witness' is nothing more spectacular than being calm and pleasant in the middle of the mayhem, but I know it makes a difference.

I've got neighbours all around me who don't half appreciate a cup of coffee and a listening ear sometimes. And I'm part of a church where my contribution is helping with the worship team.

I often say that when it comes to ministry, I'm more like Popeye than Mother Teresa. You know, 'I yam what I yam.' But with God's help I yam the best I can be. And I think I yam making a difference.
(Lara)

The demonstration of the gospel: the renewal of our world

So where do we go from here – as we walk in the company of Jesus, grow in the community of believers, engage with the culture of our times, and look to the coming of the King? We live at a time when the numerical strength of the church in the West has been decreasing. We witness a society that's torn between the pursuit of an unsatisfying consumerism and the search for an undemanding spirituality. We see a world in which the rich get richer while the poor plumb ever-greater depths of desperate poverty. Our governments face seemingly intractable problems of mounting debt, environmental disaster, diminishing natural resources, global terrorism and the breakdown of time-honoured social structures. If some throw up their hands in horror and retreat to the safety of pious separatism, that's not the way for disciples of the coming King. We must commit ourselves again to demonstrating the power of the gospel to bring renewal.

Committed to the renewal of individuals

We believe in the redemption of individuals. We must tell the story of Jesus so naturally and persuasively that men and women will discover for themselves that here is the one great story that can make sense of their stories. We may have fewer opportunities to preach than in the past, but we may have more opportunities to provoke questions by the way we live. When we respond, if our words are less condemnatory than our questioners might expect, they may well commend the grace of God more than we have been accustomed to doing. Neat and tidy evangelistic formulae that compress the gospel into four steps will be less important than encouraging people to think things through, to discover the gospel story for themselves, and to seek a personal encounter with Jesus who remains the only answer to the longings of every individual heart.

Committed to the renewal of the church

As disciples we're committed to the renewal of the church. The question is not 'Should I go to church?' but 'What kind of church do we need to become?' To seek to be a disciple without the church is like chopping off your right leg and then wondering why it doesn't run by itself and why you fall over! It functions only by being part of the body, only by realizing its dependence on every other organ, only by being fed by blood pumped from the heart, only by being directed by instructions from the brain. And the body functions only when every limb and organ plays its part. The gospel isn't just about individual salvation. It's about transformed relationships in a transformed community of people who belong together and who contribute to each other's well-being.

The church isn't identical with the kingdom of God. God's gracious rule is seen wherever his will is done. But the church should be the clearest example of the kingdom, the most vivid and colourful picture of what life looks like when people live in harmony under God's gracious rule, a glimpse of the future, a beautiful and attractive model of what life will be like when Jesus returns and the kingdom comes in all its fullness. Unless we're committed to becoming that kind of church, a watching world will miss the one thing it needs to see above everything else.

Committed to the renewal of our communities

The church doesn't exist for itself. Our primary task isn't to build bigger congregations, but to create a better world. It isn't to fill our pews with people, but to fill all creation with the glory of God. It isn't to invite people to come to church on Sunday, but to go into all the world making disciples and renewing communities every day of the week. It isn't to send the maximum number of people to heaven, but to labour and pray to bring the kingdom of heaven to earth. The opportunities to do that are all around us.

- There are kids in poorly performing schools who don't have any hope of a decent job and a solid future. *And there are disciples who are called to teach in schools like that.*
- There are old people in homes, sitting around TVs in rooms that smell of urine, and they've lost all hope and dignity. *And there are disciples who are called to work and bring transformation in homes like that.*
- There are people in council estates with dog dirt on the pavement and graffiti on the walls. They're scared to go

out after dark, and they feel hopeless about the future. *And there are disciples who are called to live and serve in estates like that.*

- There are single parents battling against the odds to bring up kids and keep them out of the gangs that threaten the very fabric of their lives. It all seems too much for them and they feel hopeless. *And there are disciples who are called to come alongside parents like that.*
- There are couples who can't make a go of their marriage. They're contemplating divorce and they can't see any hope. *And there are disciples who are called to counsel and support couples like that.*
- There are families who are deep in debt and they've no hope of sorting out their finances. *And there are disciples who are called to help and advise families like that.*
- There are addicts and alcoholics who live from one fix to the next. In their moments of clarity and sobriety they feel terrible about themselves and they haven't a hope in the world. *And there are disciples who are called to minister to addicts like that.*
- There are people who are just shy. They don't know how to make friends and normal social interaction just seems beyond them. *And there are disciples who are called to befriend people like that.*
- There are people who've done things that make them deeply ashamed and they find it hard just to live with themselves. *And there are disciples who are called to bring the good news of God's grace and forgiveness to people like that.*
- There are women and men in our prisons. Some of them are dangerous and need to be there. Others are just people with mental illness, or from broken families. *And there are disciples who are called to bring hope and dignity to prisoners like that.*

- There are people living lives that are selfish and immoral with no sense of their responsibility to others. *And there are disciples who are called to challenge them.*
- There are kids who are being abused and bullied and the adult world is a scary place for them. *And there are disciples who are called to love and mentor kids like that.*
- There are councillors and MPs struggling with massive problems and issues in our society. Often the only words they hear from the public are words of cynicism and criticism. *And there are disciples who are called not just to pray for people in public life, but to stand for office and become involved in public life.*
- There are creative people seeking to tell stories and create images that not only entertain but reach to the heart of the human condition. *And there are disciples who are gifted and called to share that work and bring the light of the gospel to bear on the world of the arts.*
- There are people whose sense of self-worth and security is bound up with their wealth and their possessions. *And there are disciples who are called to tread the dangerous path of riches, but to do it with a generosity and an awareness that they are merely stewards of God's good gifts.*
- There are millions of people whose only knowledge of the gospel is a distant memory from Sunday School days or a distorted version that only serves to turn them away from God. *And there are disciples who are called to speak truth with grace to people like that.*
- There are millions more who know even less than that about the gospel. *And there are disciples who are called to engage with them and to live in such a way that they see Jesus in us.*

The list could go on. If you take discipleship seriously, you will surely discover what God wants you to do. Your mission, should you choose to accept it, awaits you. It's a big job, bringing heaven to where you are, but you play your part in the strength of the risen Lord. And, of course, you'll have the help and support of the church, although admittedly it's a very imperfect community. Then again, if the church was perfect they wouldn't let people like you and me be part of it, would they?

Going Deeper

1. Pray through the opening lines of the Lord's Prayer:

> Our Father in heaven,
> hallowed be your name,
> your kingdom come,
> your will be done
> on earth as it is in heaven . . .

Now make a list of the places where you spend your time in any particular week. Ask yourself: What would be different if God's kingdom came and God's will was perfectly done in these places? And what part does God want me to play in bringing that about?

2. The New Testament tells us that the Jesus who will come again at 'the end' is the same Jesus who came into the world as a helpless baby two thousand years ago and who is present with his people today. What do the stories about Jesus in the Gospels and our experience of Jesus now say to us about his coming again?

Notes

Chapter 1

1. Thomas R. Kelly, *The Eternal Promise* (London: Hodder & Stoughton, 1966), p. 48.

2. David Watson, *Discipleship* (London: Hodder & Stoughton, 1981), p. 16, italics his.

3. Mark Greene, 'Imagine: How We Can Reach the UK' (London: London Institute for Contemporary Christianity, 2003), p. 4.

Chapter 2

1. The story is told by Blair's constituency agent, John Burton, in John Burton and Eileen McCabe, *We Don't Do God: Blair's Religious Belief and its Consequences* (London and New York: Continuum, 2009).

2. William Barclay, *The Daily Study Bible: The Gospel of Matthew, Vol. 2, Chapters 11 – 28* (Edinburgh: St Andrew Press, 1975), p. 151.

3. Ed Beavan, 'The Man who Took Up His Cross and Walked', *Church Times* 7632 (26 June 2009).

Chapter 3

1. Thomas à Kempis, *The Imitation of Christ*, trans. Betty I. Knott (London: Collins Fontana, 1963), p. 37.

Chapter 4

1. Interview on *ABC Good Morning America*, 4 January 2009.
2. Gary Bishop, *Darkest England: And the Way Back In* (Milton Keynes: Authentic, 2007), p. 63.
3. Ibid., p. 62.

Chapter 5

1. Justin Martyr, 'First Apology', ch. 67, taken from the New Advent website, http://www.newadvent.org/fathers/0126.htm.
2. Alexander Schmemann, *Church, World, Mission* (Crestwood, NY: St Vladimir's Seminary Press, 1979), pp. 224–225.

Chapter 6

1. Wilhelm and Marion Pauck, *Paul Tillich: His Life and Thought, Vol. 1, Life* (London: Collins, 1977), p. 283.
2. Christopher J. H. Wright, *Truth with a Mission* (Cambridge: Grove Books, 2005), p. 14.

Chapter 7

1. Stuart Murray, *Church after Christendom* (Carlisle: Paternoster, 2005), p. 220.
2. Eugene H. Peterson, *The Contemplative Pastor* (Grand Rapids: Eerdmans, 1993), quoted in the introductory interview with Rodney Clapp, p. 8.

Chapter 8

1. John A. Mackay, *God's Order: The Ephesian Letter and this Present Time*, The 1948 Croall Lectures (Nisbet & Macmillan, 1953),

quoted in John R. W. Stott, *The Message of Ephesians*, 3rd rev. ed. (Leicester: IVP, 1993), p. 124.

Chapter 9

1. Taken from the article 'Freeing Speech in a PC World', first published in *Christianity* magazine and available on the website of The London Institute for Contemporary Christianity, at http://www.licc.org.uk/engaging-with-culture/theology-of-culture/articles/freeing-speech-in-a-pc-world-966, accessed 22 January 2010.